On the Road to the Cross

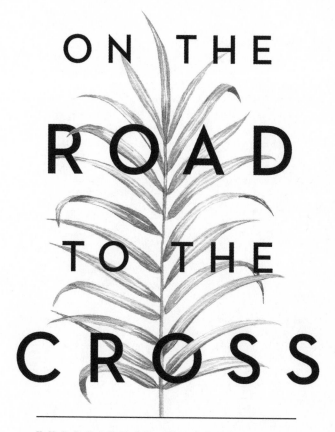

ROB BURKHART

ON THE ROAD TO THE CROSS

EXPERIENCE EASTER WITH
THOSE WHO WERE THERE

Abingdon Press

Nashville

ON THE ROAD TO THE CROSS
EXPERIENCE EASTER WITH THOSE WHO WERE THERE

Copyright © 2016 by Robin Burkhart

All rights reserved.

Library of Congress Cataloging-in-Publication Data

Names: Burkhart, Rob, author.
Title: On the road to the cross : experience Easter with those who were there / Rob Burkhart.
Description: First [edition]. | Nashville, Tennessee : Abingdon Press, 2016.
Identifiers: LCCN 2016011719 | ISBN 9781501822643 (pbk.) | 9781501822650
Subjects: LCSH: Lent—Miscellanea.
Classification: LCC BV85 .B79 2016 | DDC 232.96—dc23 LC record available at https://lccn.loc.gov/2016011719

Scripture quotations unless noted otherwise are from the Common English Bible. Copyright © 2011 by the Common English Bible. All rights reserved. Used by permission. www.CommonEnglishBible.com.

Scripture quotations marked (ESV) are from The Holy Bible, English Standard Version® (ESV®), copyright © 2001 by Crossway, a publishing ministry of Good News Publishers. Used by permission. All rights reserved.

Scripture quotations marked KJV are from The Authorized (King James) Version. Rights in the Authorized Version in the United Kingdom are vested in the Crown. Reproduced by permission of the Crown's patentee, Cambridge University Press.

16 17 18 19 20 21 22 23—10 9 8 7 6 5 4 3 2 1
MANUFACTURED IN THE UNITED STATES OF AMERICA

Contents

CONTENTS

In memory of
Paul Burkhart (1914–2002)
and
Madelyn (Still) Burkhart (1920–2015)
who rescued the future.

Acknowledgments

This book is the result of the hard work of a great cast of characters. As far as I'm concerned they are all stars!

Ann Byle of Credo Communications coached me, encouraged me, and represents my work with excellence!

Jan Rogers did what I don't do well. She helped me say what was on my heart with greater clarity and without the distractions of grammatical and technical errors.

Ramona Richards and the team at Abingdon are a delight to work with; by some alchemy I don't understand, they used their considerable skills and talents to take my thoughts and put them on bookshelves.

My thanks to Holly Halverson, who edited my final submission and made this a much better book.

I'm thankful for the lives and examples of the people whose stories are in the book who taught me more about Easter and the Christian life than they will ever know.

Finally, I am most grateful to Jesus. He knows why.

Explanations

First, the biblical stories told at the beginning of each chapter are fiction. I tried to be historically accurate and faithful to the scriptures, but no one should read them as anything but my imaginings.

Second, the personal stories at the end of each chapter really happened more or less the way they are told. In most, names were changed or omitted and details were summarized, compressed, and changed. They are told from memory. But within those limitations, they are true.

Third, some of the richness and beauty of the ancient tradition of Lent comes to us in Latin. I kept some of the Latin descriptions of each Sunday in Lent out of respect for that tradition and all the generations of believers who faithfully passed it on to us. We wouldn't know Easter without them.

Those descriptions of Lent are steps on the road to the cross and give structure to this book. On Ash Wednesday (*cinerum*) we recognize our sin. We are called (*invocabit*) into the journey to the cross and to remember (*reminiscere*) what he did for us. We see (*oculi*) the majesty of his suffering and rejoice (*laetare*) in his great love. We feel the weight of God's righteous judgment (*judica*), the hope of Palm Sunday (*dominicum palmarum*), and the agony of his passion (*pascha*) on Good Friday.

But that road doesn't end at the cross. It ends at the empty tomb.

Introduction

In film or the theater a "bit player" is a minor character who appears in a small supporting role and has at least one line of dialogue. Just because the part is small doesn't mean it isn't important. Sometimes a minor character plays the pivotal role and brings the greatest insight and meaning to a story.

Easter is full of characters who are the subjects of great literature, art, film, and music. Jesus, Judas, Peter, Pilate, Caiaphas, and Herod all assume large and impressive roles and fill the center stage of history's greatest drama. The stunning events of those days are most often told in their voices and seen from their perspective.

But minor characters are there. Easter is their story too.

The unique places of these women and men highlight elements that inspire, illuminate, and unlock the majesty of Easter. We see Easter in a new way and hear new voices when we examine their stories. Nine minor characters reveal, in bold strokes and vivid colors, truths that easily elude the casual reader but when discovered speak eloquently into our lives, hopes, and fears.

Just a few days before his death, Jesus attended a dinner in Bethany hosted by Simon the Leper. That night Mary, the sister of Lazarus and Martha, anointed his feet. Another day, Jesus visited the home of Simon the Pharisee in Capernaum and, there, was anointed by a "sinful woman." Together these stories remind us that Jesus included and welcomed all who came to him.

Malchus came to the garden of Gethsemane an enemy of Christ and suffered the painful consequences of that choice. But Malchus found healing in the touch of the man he came to harm.

The centurion faced a crisis of truth at the foot of the cross. His is a story of the struggle within when the truth we know is at war with the lives we live.

On the road to nowhere, Cleopas and his companion encountered Christ and discovered a truth that changed the direction of their lives. We are all on a road to discover our place in the world and ourselves.

Nicodemus and Joseph of Arimathea pretended to be what they weren't and were forced to choose a path. Those who hide behind carefully created facades ultimately face a crisis of identity and integrity.

Barabbas deserved punishment but got a last-minute reprieve. Another took his place and carried his cross. Pilate, who released Barabbas and condemned Jesus, was a prisoner to his fears and ambitions. He lived with the illusion of freedom. We are all prisoners, whether we recognize it or not, looking for freedom.

Simon the Cyrene was a bystander on the Via Dolorosa. Fate and a Roman soldier intervened to make him an active participant in the events of that day. We all decide whether we live as spectators or fully participate in life's greatest adventure.

Mary Magdalene stood at the foot of the cross and watched her dreams die. Three days later she witnessed the beginning of a new reality and the resurrection of her dreams.

Everyone wants a better life now. One may accept or reject the death and resurrection of Christ and its implications for everlasting life. But the hunger for a richer, fuller life now binds all of us together.

The world's other great religions promise new life after death in paradise or reincarnation. Christianity alone promises new life now, in this world and in the next, for all those who come to the one who conquered death that first

Easter morning. Jesus taught that we can be "born again" and get a second chance. Resurrection life is for the here and now, not just the there and then.

What if we could find a place in this life where we were truly accepted and could live open and authentic lives? What if we could be free from the prisons of our past and our pain? What if there was an end to the restless searching and a discovery of a place where dreams come true? What if we could fully engage life with all its wonder, mystery, and adventure?

Wouldn't that be worth the journey to the cross?

Chapter 1

The Leper and the Prostitute

Cinerum
Ash Wednesday

Memento, homo, quia pulvis es, et in pulverem reverteris
For dust thou art, and unto dust shalt thou return.

Genesis 3:19 (KJV)

Et emisit eum Dominus Deus de paradiso voluptatis . . . Ejecitque Adam
Therefore the Lord God sent him forth from the garden of Eden, . . . So
he drove out the man.

Genesis 3:23-24a (KJV)

*No man is excluded from calling upon God, the gate of salvation is set open
unto all men: neither is there any other thing which keepeth us back from
entering in, save only our own unbelief.*
—John Calvin

The Leper's Request

"Unclean! Unclean!" the leper shouted as he approached a small group of men. He kept the Law's instruction to warn people of his approach so they could avoid close contact.

The men stopped and eyed the leper cautiously, careful to keep their distance.

"I'm looking for the Rabbi—the one from Capernaum. I heard he was teaching near here. People say he can heal. Do you know where he is? I've come all the way from Bethany to find him."

The men looked at each other. Then one spoke up.

"We were there. He finished teaching and is coming down the mountain. It's not far. If you hurry you can catch him," the man said and pointed to the top of a nearby hill.

"He lives in Capernaum but he's from Nazareth," another man said.

"How will I know him?" It seemed like a reasonable question, but the men chuckled.

"Don't worry. You'll know him."

"Thank you!" Simon the Leper shouted as he struggled toward the hilltop.

The men watched Simon go.

"Do you think the Rabbi will heal him? He's a leper," one of them said.

"I don't know. That Rabbi isn't like the Pharisees. Sometimes he breaks the rules."

"I heard he let a prostitute anoint his feet when he was at a Pharisee's house in Capernaum, and he forgave her sins," added a third man.

"Who knows what he'll do?"

When he crested the hill, Simon saw him. The man was right. There was no mistaking the Rabbi. The Rabbi and his disciples moved slowly away from

3

him. Panic gripped Simon. He had come too far and had too much at stake to let this opportunity slip away.

He pulled up his long robe and carefully made his way down the hill. Near the bottom he tripped and fell in the dirt and rocks. Bruised and scraped, he got up and began again. The Rabbi and his disciples noticed the commotion, stopped, and turned toward the leper who

> fell on his face and begged, "Lord, if you want, you can make me clean." Jesus reached out his hand, touched him, and said, "I do want to. Be clean." Instantly, the skin disease left him. Jesus ordered him not to tell anyone. "Instead," Jesus said, "go and show yourself to the priest and make an offering for your cleansing, as Moses instructed. This will be a testimony to them." (Luke 5:12-14)

Simon did exactly what the Rabbi said: he went to the nearest village and showed himself to a priest. The old man inspected every inch of his body before declaring him clean. Clean! The priest helped him make his thanksgiving offering, buy new clothes, bathe, get something to eat, and get a room at the inn.

When he woke, the village buzzed with the story of his healing. The Rabbi had asked him not to talk about it, and he'd told only the priest. The priest told everyone!

Simon went by the priest's home to thank him and say good-bye.

"What's next? Are you going to follow him too?" the priest asked.

"No. My wife is expecting and I have a young son at home. I'd follow the Rabbi or do something for him if I could. Maybe I'll get the chance someday, but I'm going home!"

Days later Simon the Leper walked down the dusty road to Bethany and approached his house. His wife, Anna, saw him through the window, scooped up their young son, Joshua, and ran to him. They were together again and happy. He hugged her and held her close. Joshua grinned and giggled when Simon tossed him in the air. Their reunion was his dream come true.

That afternoon Simon visited his friend Lazarus, Martha and Mary's brother, to thank him for looking after Anna and Joshua while he was gone and to tell him about the miracle.

Simon said, "Maybe he'll come by on his way to Jerusalem for one of the festivals. I told him I lived in Bethany and that he and his disciples were welcome anytime. If he comes I'll introduce you to him. I think you'll like him."

Simon the Leper and the Anointing at Bethany

Matthew 26:6-15; Mark 14:1-11; John 12:1-11

Six days before Passover, Jesus came to Bethany, home of Lazarus, whom Jesus had raised from the dead. Lazarus and his sisters hosted a dinner for him. Martha served and Lazarus was among those who joined him at the table. (John 12:1-2)

Jesus was at Bethany visiting the house of Simon, who had a skin disease. During dinner, a woman came in with a vase made of alabaster and containing very expensive perfume of pure nard. She broke open the vase and poured the perfume on his head. (Mark 14:3)

Before the great drama of redemption played out in an upper room, a garden, the streets of Jerusalem and Golgotha, Jesus went to Bethany. The village, about a mile and a half west of Jerusalem, was close enough for easy access to the city but far enough away that Jesus could rest and relax. He was among friends who believed in him, welcomed him, and supported him.

Two days before Christ's triumphal entry, his friends hosted a dinner for him and his disciples at the house of Simon the Leper. It was an odd mixture of people—as odd as one can imagine. Lazarus, back from the dead, was there. Simon, cured from an incurable disease, was there. Judas Iscariot, whose plot to betray Christ was already in motion, was there. And, as strange as it seems, Christ's critics and opponents were there ready to take offense, find fault, and criticize. Admirers and antagonists gathered at the same table, watched the same drama unfold, and saw completely different truths. Martha was there serving. Mary and her alabaster flask of perfumed nard waited in the wings.

> Then Mary took an extraordinary amount, almost three-quarters of a pound, of very expensive perfume made of pure nard. She anointed Jesus' feet with it, then wiped his feet dry with her hair. The house was filled with the aroma of the perfume. (John 12:3)

Jesus was there.

The Sinful Woman and the Anointing at Capernaum

Luke 7:36-50

The accounts of Christ's anointing at Bethany and Capernaum are often confused. But these events occurred at different times in Christ's ministry, in different places, and with a different cast of characters.

Jesus focused much of his early ministry in and around Capernaum. His teaching and miraculous ministry attracted the attention of both followers and detractors. He was invited to and attended a dinner hosted by Simon the Pharisee, who treated him disrespectfully.

> One of the Pharisees invited Jesus to eat with him. After he entered the Pharisee's home, he took his place at the table. (Luke 7:36)

> When I entered your home, you didn't give me water for my feet. . . . You didn't greet me with a kiss. . . . You didn't anoint my head with oil. (Luke 7:44-46)

At that dinner a "sinful woman" anointed Christ's feet with oil.

> Meanwhile, a woman from the city, a sinner, discovered that Jesus was dining in the Pharisee's house. She brought perfumed oil in a vase made of alabaster. Standing behind him at his feet and crying, she began to wet his feet with her tears. She wiped them with her hair, kissed them, and poured the oil on them. (Luke 7:37-38)

The encounter demonstrated Christ's willing acceptance of all who came to him, whether they were broken by or blinded to their own sin.

In both Capernaum and Bethany, Christ encountered society's excluded as well as its privileged and powerful. That divide was deeply entrenched. Ethnicity, education, lifestyle, wealth, religion, and power were boundary lines for them as they often are for us.

In both places, Christ displayed the grandeur of inclusive grace and revealed the poverty of exclusive religion. The deepest truths of Easter, the core issues of life and faith, stand in bold relief in the stories of a leper and a prostitute.

Included

In the anointing accounts, we see that Jesus was the most inclusive, least judgmental, and most welcoming person in history. He crossed ethnic, socioeconomic, gender, and religious boundaries and went out of his way to receive people whom the powerful and privileged rejected. He welcomed them, valued them, spent time with them, and enjoyed their company.

Christ's genuine acceptance of people whom others rejected happened so often that it is impossible to miss. He did not approve of their pasts, their current lifestyles, or their future bad acts. In fact he taught the opposite. But when they came, Christ freed them—when they were willing—from their self-destructive lives so they could experience his love, forgiveness, and grace.

Christ Welcomed the Unwelcome

Jesus did what most people can't: he upheld the highest moral standards and made people feel cared for and accepted at the same time. Jesus did not confuse people with their pasts or equate them with their failures. He never pointed out where and how they failed. They already knew. Love and acceptance create an opportunity for transformation while criticism and condemnation petrify the soul.

Society's outcasts welcomed Jesus into their hearts, their homes, and their lives. Again and again we find Jesus in places and with people whom others had rejected. He socialized with tax collectors, publicans, and sinners. These imperfect people felt most comfortable in the presence of the one perfect man.

Christ Valued People

Regardless of their lifestyles or their pasts, Jesus saw them for what they were: divine image bearers broken by sin, burdened by religion, banished from society. They were the very people he came to seek and save (Luke 19:10). He saw them through the eyes of grace.

All too often we measure others by the wrong standard. We deem others valuable based on whether or not they contribute positively to our lives, the lives of others, or society as a whole. If they don't, we don't value them. We don't even really see them.

Jesus did. For example, he knew that the women's gifts were costly and that giving them was risky. He knew they were natural and heartfelt expressions of their love and devotion, not efforts to cajole or manipulate him. He valued the women and their selfless gifts.

Christ Valued Sacrifice

The banquet at Bethany demanded sacrifice. We don't know who paid for the feast. Maybe it was Simon or Lazarus or both. But somebody paid. We don't know how many people attended, but Martha and others sacrificially served. The flask of perfume Mary poured out with such reckless joy was extremely expensive. At the end of the dinner, all she had was a broken flask and a sweet aroma.

Here is a simple and elegant truth: those who truly know and truly love Christ lose themselves in him. The epicenter of life shifts. Life orbits a different Son. It ceases to be an endless self-centered pursuit and becomes a joy-filled and selfless journey. Jesus values this kind of sacrifice.

Christ Inspired Love

In the stories of Jesus's anointing at Capernaum we may wonder: why did a woman judged the worst kind of person of her time explode with such an extravagant act of love while the religious and self-righteous disdained and criticized her?

> When the Pharisee who had invited Jesus saw what was happening, he said to himself, If this man were a prophet, he would know what kind of woman is touching him. He would know that she is a sinner.
>
> Jesus replied, "Simon, I have something to say to you."
>
> "Teacher, speak," he said.
>
> "A certain lender had two debtors. One owed enough money to pay five hundred people for a day's work. The other owed enough money for fifty. When they couldn't pay, the lender forgave the debts of them both. Which of them will love him more?"
>
> Simon replied, "I suppose the one who had the largest debt canceled."
>
> Jesus said, "You have judged correctly." (Luke 7:39-43)

Love and forgiveness are forever linked. The outcast's lavish gratitude was the direct result of the expansive forgiveness and love she was given. She knew the depths of her depravity and the misery of her sin. She celebrated Jesus's welcome and grace because she had experienced the pain caused by the people who sneered and snarled at her.

Christ's critics didn't rejoice with the sinful woman because they were blind to their own need. Some people are just as blind today. As Jesus explained:

> "This is why I tell you that her many sins have been forgiven; so she has shown great love. The one who is forgiven little loves little." Then Jesus said to her, "Your sins are forgiven." The other table guests began to say among themselves, "Who is this person that even forgives sins?" Jesus said to the woman, "Your faith has saved you. Go in peace." (Luke 7:47-50)

Grace is, always has been, and always will be fundamentally unfair. It's an old saying, trite but true: justice gives what people deserve. Mercy doesn't give people all they deserve. But grace gives people what they don't deserve. Jesus's grace stood the entire religious and social system of his day on its head. It still does. And it still inspires acts of great love.

Christ Invested

He talked at length to the Samaritan woman at the well (John 4:1-45) and went home with Zacchaeus the tax collector (Luke 19:1-10). He touched lepers (Luke 5:12-16), allowed delivered demoniacs to sit at his feet (Luke 8:2; Mark 5:1-20), healed the Roman centurion's servant (Luke 7:1-10), and brought society's marginalized and rejected (a leper and a sinful woman) into his inner circle. Everywhere he went people were drawn to him.

Jesus is still a friend of the rejected, ostracized, and marginalized. He still welcomes imperfect and broken people. We discover that life need not be defined by our worst moments. He transforms our broken pasts into our best lives by the power of love and grace.

We who have been welcomed are called to welcome others, value them, inspire them, and invest in their futures whether or not they are like us, it's easy, or they live up to our expectations. That is, if we want to be like Jesus.

The Powerful and Privileged

The powerful and privileged kept their distance and ultimately tried to destroy Jesus and his followers. Why?

In the bright light of his true righteousness the moral poverty of petty rule-keeping is clear. What his critics were most proud of added up to nothing that truly mattered. Rule-keeping didn't create happiness, joy, or satisfaction, and it didn't bring value to the world. The Pharisees and self-righteous pursued trivia. The last thing they wanted was to stand in the glare of the one man who lived without sin and with real love, real grace, and real purpose.

They were prisoners of a system forged by their predecessors and trapped in an endless maze of ridiculous rules that governed every aspect of life. It rewarded them with status, power, and prestige. But they completely missed the point. What they valued was of no value to God, and what God valued most was of little or no value to them. No wonder they hated Jesus. No wonder some still do.

Jesus disrupted their well-ordered society, erased their lines, and redefined all the categories. Poor and generous was better than rich and grandiose (Luke 21:1-4). A brokenhearted tax collector begging for forgiveness was better than his self-righteous religious critic (Luke 18:9-14). Repentant prostitutes, lepers, demoniacs, gentiles, the ignorant, the poor, and the sinner were welcome in the kingdom of God before the unrepentant religious elite.

Some people still keep their distance from the radical, disruptive truths of love and acceptance Christ proclaimed. They turn his teachings into an excuse to act like those who don't follow him. Hiding behind religious rituals and regulations, they misrepresent his teaching and exclude, demean, and sometimes hate the people Jesus loves and died for. They are more like the people who killed Jesus than like Jesus.

Tough Love

And yet it is a monumental mistake to think that Jesus loved the powerful and privileged less than those they ostracized. He didn't. He responded to the outcasts as he did because he loved them so much and they got it—they knew who and what they were and reached out for his love, mercy, and forgiveness.

Jesus responded to the powerful and privileged as he did because he loved them so much and they didn't get it—at all! It broke his heart.

At the banquet hosted by Simon the Leper, Judas's criticisms of Mary were dishonest. He lied about his motives and feigned concern for the poor. Judas was angered because he missed the opportunity to steal from Jesus and the others. He wanted those gathered for dinner to see him as something he wasn't.

> Judas Iscariot . . . complained, "This perfume was worth a year's wages! Why wasn't it sold and the money given to the poor?" (He said this not because he cared about the poor but because he was a thief. He carried the money bag and would take what was in it.) Then Jesus said, "Leave her alone. This perfume was to be used in preparation for my burial, and this is how she has used it." (John 12:4-7)

Some of those watching the anointings at Capernaum and Bethany were dishonest and deceitful. Some said to themselves indignantly, "Why was the ointment wasted like that?" Others were dishonest but silent. We don't know why they were indignant or why they were silent. Perhaps they resented Mary's act of worship. Perhaps they were just cowards.

Some were neither dishonest nor deceptive. They were destructive. Angered by Mary's gift, they attacked, demeaned, and publicly humiliated her rather than celebrate with her or admire her generosity: "And they scolded her" (Mark 14:4-5).

Have you noticed that those who come to Christ rarely get religious rituals or customs right? They don't act, talk, or dress the way others think they should. How could they? They don't know the rules and have no reason to care about them. Sometimes they meet dishonest, deceptive, or destructive people and feel demeaned and criticized. It shouldn't happen. But it does.

Jesus knew who his critics truly were. Judas was the greedy thief who would betray him for the price of a slave. Simon was a self-righteous and hypocritical Pharisee who would deny Jesus the most common courtesies. Others were there to challenge, trick, or humiliate him.

But Jesus didn't reject them; instead he practiced tough love. Confront them? Yes. Challenge them? Certainly. Push them to self-examination and repentance. Without a doubt! Anger them to the point of murderous rage? Absolutely. Reject them? Never! Any of them, like Nicodemus and Joseph of Arimathea, could have abandoned their empty, miserable, self-righteous lives and followed him. He never rejected them. They rejected him.

Jesus challenged the powerful and privileged directly, clearly, and sometimes painfully. He loved them too much to let them continue to believe the rubbish they spouted. He wanted to free them from the slavery of meaningless rule-keeping and to enjoy the liberty of true righteousness. Sometimes Jesus seemed harsh. Clearly, he wasn't one to mince words. He was as tough and forceful as the situation and the people he confronted demanded. But it was always with a heart of love and a desire to include them too.

The more hard-hearted a person becomes the more likely it is they will experience God's tough love. God may let them experience the miserable consequences of their own choices because he loves them, wants them to turn to him and discover the greatest joys of life in his presence.

A Different View

Simon the Pharisee saw a prostitute touch a Rabbi and was outraged. The Jews at Bethany saw the waste of a resource that could have been put to better use. Jesus saw it all from a completely different perspective.

> Jesus turned to the woman and said to Simon, "Do you see this woman? When I entered your home, you didn't give me water for my feet, but she wet my feet with tears and wiped them with her hair. You didn't greet me with a kiss, but she hasn't stopped kissing my feet since I came in. You didn't anoint my head with oil, but she has poured perfumed oil on my feet. This is why I tell you that her many sins have been forgiven; so she has shown great love. The one who is forgiven little loves little."
>
> Then Jesus said to her, "Your sins are forgiven." (Luke 7:44-48)

We are prone to judge others and events in terms of our own perceptions and react accordingly. What the critics needed and what we need is Christ's perspective. He looked beyond the natural and saw the spiritual, beyond the immediate impact and saw the true significance.

In Capernaum, Christ's honor wasn't at stake, nor was becoming ceremonially unclean. The prostitute's trespass in Simon the Pharisee's house wasn't the issue either. Those things were true enough in the moment. But what mattered most was her act of faith and that one broken, suffering woman was redeemed and restored by the glorious power of God's love.

Mary's flask of perfumed ointment didn't matter. The fate of hungry people wasn't really at stake. The culmination of God's eternal plan for human redemption was at hand. A new era of God's grace and forgiveness free from ethnic identity and vain religion was bursting on the scene. The cold stench of sin's death grip would forever yield to the aroma of salvation. That's what mattered.

Sometimes we get it wrong too. Some people still value their church buildings and traditions more than they value the people who gather to worship or those who never come to church. Some people still think that compassion or working for a just society is all that really matters. Mary and the sinful woman in Capernaum teach us something very different. The two aren't at odds with each other. They are different expressions of the same thing. True worship and true compassion flow from the same source: love for Christ and devotion to his cause.

In the End

There is no doubt: the impulse to exclude people exists today. Those who wish to be inclusive sometimes confuse loving and accepting people with approving of their behavior. They think that holding fast to a doctrine, a practice, or a lifestyle means excluding those who disagree or whose lifestyles they find offensive. It's a false dichotomy. We don't have to and shouldn't choose between loving and accepting people and living a lifestyle that honors God. Jesus loved people, led a sinless life, and never approved of or endorsed wrongdoing. We can and should do the same.

Easter belongs to everyone. Ethnicity, education, wealth, status, and power don't matter. Easter belongs to the ostracized and sinners, to the self-righteous and the religious, to the disinterested and the disheartened. It belongs to all of us because Jesus loves and welcomes all who come. It doesn't matter whether we come to worship, to question, or to struggle. All are welcome, just like the leper and the prostitute.

The Chair, 1975

March 23—Palm Sunday
March 28—Good Friday
March 30—Easter Sunday

I reached up and took the old chair from the hook on the back wall of the carport. I thought about getting rid of it, but I just couldn't bring myself to toss it in the Dumpster. It was mute testimony to the chair's incredible ugliness that it hung in an open carport for months and no one took it. Apparently it wasn't even worth stealing.

The chair was a gift from my grandfather on the day my new wife and I moved to California. It sat on his front porch for more years than I could remember and had been painted and repainted every time Grandpa had some leftover paint. It was so ugly we didn't want to have it in the house.

My brother suggested I strip off the paint and refinish the chair. Maybe it was salvageable. If not, I could always get rid of it.

I worked all day stripping layer after layer of paint from the chair. I counted eleven. The last layer was white. When I finally got down to the wood I was shocked. The chair was handcrafted solid oak. The natural grain of the wood was gorgeous. The layers of paint obscured beautiful, intricate scrollwork.

It took me several days to complete the project, to sand and scrub the chair with steel wool until it was as smooth as silk and not a speck of paint remained, to reglue the joints, to apply a light oil to restore the luster, and then to add several coats of a clear finish to protect the wood. When I finished, I stepped back and admired a true treasure. I had been very wrong. It had been ugly only on the outside. Underneath was all the beauty of its maker.

Just like most people. Just like my grandfather.

The chair moved inside that day and has had a prominent place in every home we have owned.

When we went for a visit I brought pictures of the chair for Grandpa to see. "Where did you get the chair?" I asked.

"I bought it at a church auction . . . paid fifty cents for it. It's the pulpit chair from that church your mother went to when she was a little girl. I figured a preacher needed his own pulpit chair," was his matter-of-fact reply.

Chapter 2

The Walking Wounded

Invocabit

1st Sunday in Lent

Introit
Invocavit me et exaudiam eum.
He shall call upon me, and I will answer him.
Psalm 91:15 (KJV)

Because he hath set his love upon me, therefore will I deliver him: I will set him
on high, because he hath known my name.
He shall call upon me, and I will answer him: I will be with him in trouble; I
will deliver him, and honor him.
With long life will I satisfy him, and shew him my salvation.
Psalm 91:14-16 (KJV)

Here bring your wounded hearts; here tell your anguish;
Earth has no sorrow that Heaven cannot heal.
—Thomas Moore

Malchus Remembers

The boy got caught rummaging through his grandfather's things. Just as he pulled back the coarse sleeping mat and saw a carefully wrapped oblong package, his grandfather spoke from the doorway. "Can I help you find something?"

His grandfather knelt down and carefully untied the strings and opened the bundle. First he took out the finest robe the boy had ever seen. Elegantly embroidered, it was fit for someone very rich and powerful. When the old man held it up in the dim light the boy could see that the right shoulder was covered in a dark stain that ran down the sleeve to the cuff.

"See the stain? That's my blood. I was wearing this the night a man named Peter cut off my ear and a man named Jesus healed me," he said to the boy.

The old man put down the robe and picked up the other object—a Roman short sword—and handed it to the boy.

"Peter gave it to me," said the old man. "He said it would help me remember what happened that night. As if I could ever forget.

"Do you want to hear the story?"

"Yes, Grandpa."

"It all happened long before you were born.

"I was a leader of the temple guard in Jerusalem. During Passover we were sent to arrest a man named Jesus who claimed to be the Messiah. Judas, one of his disciples, betrayed him. Judas didn't want to go but we made him take us to him. It was part of the deal. I led the temple guards and a Roman centurion and his soldiers through the dark streets, outside the city, and into a garden called Gethsemane.

"The Rabbi was praying with his disciples.

25

"I couldn't believe it: Judas walked right up and kissed the Rabbi.

"Then I stepped up to arrest the Rabbi.

"It happened so fast. I didn't see the big man reach under his cloak and pull out his sword. I remember the flash of the blade in the torchlight. I turned my head and tried to get out of the way. But I wasn't quick enough. The tip of the blade caught my right ear and cut it off. Well, not all the way. It dangled by a little piece of skin. It didn't hurt much at first—shock, I guess. Then it hurt a lot!

"I thought there was going to be an all-out battle. My soldiers and the Romans were yelling and pulling their swords. But that's not what happened.

"'Stop, enough of this!' the Rabbi shouted.

"He told the man to put the sword away. Well, there I stood covered with blood, holding my ear. Then the Rabbi reached out.

"I still remember the look on his face. He wasn't angry. He should have been but he wasn't. He looked as if he felt everything I felt and really cared. He reached up and pulled my hand away and touched my ear. I didn't feel anything. Well, I felt something but I can't explain it. Suddenly it was as if nothing had happened. My face didn't hurt. I wasn't bleeding and my ear was back where it was supposed to be. The cut was completely healed. It wasn't until the next day that I noticed the scar."

The old man turned his head so his grandson could get a better look and ran his finger along a jagged scar obscured by his beard. It stretched from the top of his ear to the edge of his jaw.

"We arrested him. They tried him that night and crucified him the next morning. It was awful.

"Three days later I heard rumors that he had come back from the dead. The temple guards made up a story that they had fallen asleep and his disciples stole the body. I knew those men. It was all a lie.

"So I looked for his followers.

"It took some doing but I found the big man who cut off my ear. He was afraid at first. After a while he introduced me to the rest of the Rabbi's followers. They'd all seen the Rabbi—alive. I didn't believe it. Of course neither did they at first. But I was there when he appeared to them. I saw him too. He was alive. He recognized me. Don't ask me how. It was so dark and confusing that night. When he saw me he smiled, gave a little tug on his right ear, and winked.

"I saw him ascend into heaven. I was in the upper room in Jerusalem the day it happened. I heard the wind. I saw the flames. It's all . . . well . . . it's all *real*. He is the Messiah, the Christ. I know that now. I arrested him and helped them torture and kill him and what did he do? Heal me. Forgive me. Love me.

"It didn't take long for the persecution to start. Thousands of people believed in the Rabbi, and the religious leaders wanted it stopped. They thought it would end when they killed him. I guess they didn't count on him coming back from the dead.

"No one did."

Malchus, the High Priest's Servant

Matthew 26:47-56; Mark 14:43-50; Luke 22:47-51; John 18:1-12

The world is awash in the walking wounded. They wander the great battlefields of life suffering physical, mental, emotional, and spiritual wounds. Sometimes their wounds aren't obvious but that doesn't mean they suffer less.

We don't know much about Malchus. He was a servant of the high priest and was in the garden of Gethsemane that night to arrest Christ and carry out the orders of legitimate authority. Malchus was within reach of Peter's sword and Christ's touch. He may have been the instrument of an evil plot, but it wasn't his plot. Malchus was in the wrong place at the wrong time and was suddenly and savagely attacked.

> His betrayer had given them a sign: "Arrest the man I kiss." Just then he came to Jesus and said, "Hello, Rabbi." Then he kissed him.
> But Jesus said to him, "Friend, do what you came to do." Then they came and grabbed Jesus and arrested him. (Matthew 26:48-50)

> Then Simon Peter, who had a sword, drew it and struck the high priest's servant, cutting off his right ear. (The servant's name was Malchus.) (John 18:10)

Malchus and Peter faced each other across a great divide. As far as Malchus was concerned, Jesus and his followers were a dangerous and deluded sect. Malchus and those with him were under orders from the high priest, who had the best interests of the nation in mind. Their actions were legal, right, and practically necessary.

To Peter, Malchus and all those with him were enemies. They threatened Peter's friend, his future, and God's plans to redeem all of humankind. Jesus fulfilled divine prophecy, was the answer to centuries of Jewish questions, and proved his divinity again and again by the brilliance of his teaching, his miracles, and his incredible life.

Peter and Malchus met where adversaries always meet: we wound and are wounded on one of life's many battlefields. Those wounds are horribly painful and strike at the very heart of our identities, if not of our bodies. We have all done it and had it done to us.

Malchus threatened what was precious to Peter. Surrounded by a superior force with no place to run, Peter protected his Messiah. He attacked to defend a cherished relationship, a longed-for future, and his own life. Malchus, who embodied that threat, was the object of his attack, and he suffered for it.

Protecting what we love is a deep and primal instinct. In that split second of blind rage, nothing exists except our pain and fear—and God help whoever is in the way. We don't think about the consequences. It doesn't matter if the threat is real or not. Sometimes we completely misunderstand and create innocent victims by striking out at people who are not trying to hurt us. We just think they are.

Sometimes we hit back in a rage or we run from the pain and abandon them. Sometimes we self-medicate, trying to drown the pain. Sometimes we find solace in another. Sometimes we destroy what the other loves. We inflict agony on those who knowingly or unknowingly touch us where it hurts.

Malchus took an aggressive posture and laid hands on Jesus (Matthew 26:50). More than his presence, more than the threatening nature of his mission, his aggressive act brought on Peter's attack.

Armed and Dangerous

Before the shocking night in Gethsemane, the disciples had just enjoyed the Last Supper. Men with concealed weapons aren't part of our image of the Last Supper. We think of Christ's humility as he knelt to wash his disciples' feet, the beauty and grandeur of his words and actions that became the pivotal and quintessential Christian rite, the Eucharist, or we remember DaVinci's magnificent painting; not violent men.

But prior to the bloody confrontation and arrest, we read that Jesus went to the garden of Gethsemane to pray. Peter went ready for a skirmish.

> They said to him, "Lord, look, here are two swords." He replied, "Enough of that!" (Luke 22:38)

It's hard to imagine the disciples diligently working whetstones until their swords were razor sharp. It's at odds with the attitude of the one who taught the world to turn the other cheek. It doesn't fit with their gentle teacher, the prince of peace, or the future leaders of a great spiritual movement at a seminal moment in Christian history.

Nor is it how we think about the garden of Gethsemane. Sleepy disciples? Yes. Agonizing prayer? Yes. Incredible love and grace as Christ submitted to the will of the Father and his coming fate? Yes. His disciples ready to kill and maim his enemies? Yes (see Luke 22:49). The disciples expected trouble and were prepared for a battle they couldn't win.

Some people are always ready for a fight.

A Very Human Response

When they saw the light of the torches coming their way, Peter and the others knew what would happen. It's easy to see Peter slipping his hand under his cloak and gripping the hilt of the sword carefully hidden among its folds. His attack seems justifiable, even heroic. Facing overwhelming odds with little or no chance of victory, Peter risked his life to save his friend.

Like so many others, Peter saw the world in terms of conflict and confrontation. Such people are ready for a fight, ready to defend themselves and if necessary to destroy the opposition. People still believe that attacking someone and inflicting pain and suffering are justified. That's a questionable premise.

Malchus didn't matter. Peter didn't see him as another person or think about his wife or children and what would happen to them if Malchus died under his sword. Peter's fear and the rightness of his cause blinded him to the larger implications of his actions.

Peter is like us. When threatened, we don't think. We lose sight of the value of the other person and forget that they suffer too. Our actions open ugly wounds that may never truly heal. Then they and we live with the miserable downstream results.

We most often attack not with fists, swords, or guns, but with words. But we kill all the same. We kill our relationships, our victims' sense of value, and the future that could have been. Damaged and disfigured, our victims become walking wounded, suffering silently while their great pain hides in some dark recess of the soul. Thick, ugly scars left by the searing pain of our attacks mark their minds, their emotions, and their souls.

On that night Jesus had something else in mind, something incomprehensible to all who hide their swords in the cloak of civility.

The Atypical Response

We understand Malchus. We've all been innocent victims of an attack that left us wounded and hurting. We understand Peter. We've all lashed out at someone in a moment of fear and pain. What we don't understand, what is beyond our experience and the way of the world, what is so atypical it's hard to believe, is Christ's response.

Jesus had the most to fear and the unchallenged right to anger; he'd experienced the intense pain of betrayal and had the greatest ability to protect himself. But he turned his back on what most believe is legitimate, expected, and normal. He refused to fight back. It seems contrary to common sense.

But grace isn't at all common. Perhaps if we dealt with pain his way instead of ours, we could change the world.

But there is a caveat.

Evil exists. No one truly doubts it. Some see it embodied in a personal spiritual force, the devil and his demons. Others believe it is an aberration or a sickness. Some think it is learned or the result of wounds left untreated. Regardless of its source, monstrous evil prowls the earth, sometimes on two legs and with a human form and face.

What are we to do when an evil exists that cannot be reasoned with, will not stop, and cannot be tolerated? The answer is simple and straightforward: such evil must be stopped. Hitler would have continued to exterminate European Jewry and all those he believed were unfit had he not been stopped. The horrors inflicted on the people of Cambodia by Pol Pot, the monstrosities in Kosova, Rwanda, and myriad other places had to be stopped.

Serial killers and rapists, child predators, and a host of others can't be cajoled, coddled, or convinced to quit preying on others. The best society can do is stop them. Sometimes that means prison; sometimes it's the execution-er's needle or a police officer's bullet. Sadly only an act of violence ends their violence.

But most of us don't deal with these extremes.

Christ's way wasn't *kill or be killed, maim or be maimed*. Christ demon-strated seven principles of dealing with the attacks we face that bring healing and wholeness.

1. Just Stop

Jesus responded, "Stop! No more of this!" (Luke 22:51)

Somebody, somewhere, sometime has to say enough is enough and put an end to the ever-escalating cycle of retaliation and pain. It takes great com-passion, courage, and wisdom to call an end to hostilities when every instinct tells us to hit back as hard as we can. It is amazingly brave to take the blow and refuse to escalate the conflict. But if it can be done, new and fantastic possibil-ities emerge. There is hope.

A sensitive answer turns back wrath, but an offensive word stirs up anger. (Proverbs 15:1)

2. Disarm

Then Jesus said to him, "Put the sword back into its place. All those who use the sword will die by the sword." (Matthew 26:52)

The sword that dripped with Malchus's blood was in Peter's hand. He was still dangerous and more than capable of attacking again. Even though the sol-diers and temple guards bristled with weapons, Jesus demanded unilateral dis-armament. Peter was to put his sword away whether or not his adversaries did.

All of us know someone who lives with a "sword" at the ready. We may have handed them the weapon they wield against us. Our failures, mistakes, and blunders are stockpiled like ammunition. What causes us pain, threatens us, and terrifies us is within easy reach. Our adversaries may not be on the attack but they certainly have not disarmed. It's not war. But it's certainly not peace.

Pulling down our defenses and laying aside our weapons makes us vulnerable and feels dangerous. But it's the only way. We cannot expect others to disarm if we are still a threat.

The route to disarmament is the way of love. Perhaps the apostle Paul said it best when he wrote these cherished words:

> Love is patient, love is kind, it isn't jealous, it doesn't brag, it isn't arrogant, it isn't rude, it doesn't seek its own advantage, it isn't irritable, it doesn't keep a record of complaints, it isn't happy with injustice, but it is happy with the truth. Love puts up with all things, trusts in all things, hopes for all things, endures all things. (1 Corinthians 13:4-7)

3. Don't Retaliate

> "Or do you think that I'm not able to ask my Father and he will send to me more than twelve battle groups of angels right away?" (Matthew 26:53)

Jesus could have called his Father's angels to wreak havoc on Judas, Malchus, and the soldiers. The principle is clear: ultimate justice isn't found in this world or by human means. It certainly isn't found in blood feuds. True justice is in the hands of God, who will make all things right in the end. People retaliate because they fear the wrong done to them will go unpunished. They don't trust God to make it right.

4. Live for a Greater Purpose

"But if I did that, how then would the scriptures be fulfilled that say this must happen?" (Matthew 26:54)

What was in front of Peter was all that mattered. He did not see or understand that this horrific moment and the tragedy that would unfold in the next twenty-four hours had significance far beyond the events themselves. It was part of a much greater plan to redeem humankind. God would transform this travesty into the most magnificent truth in human history. Jesus threw himself into a future that Peter could not see and into the arms of a God whom Peter did not yet know. Underlying Christ's actions was a deep and resolute trust in his Father.

5. Know That Victimizers Are Also Victims

[Jesus] touched [Malchus's] ear and healed him. (Luke 22:51)

The interaction between Jesus, Malchus, and Peter is telling. Jesus was an innocent victim of a friend's betrayal and a cruel plot. He did nothing to deserve his arrest, the sham trial, or the cruel torture and crucifixion that awaited him.

Malchus and the men with him intended to—and in the end succeeded to—victimize Jesus. Their actions led to a horror few can truly comprehend.

Peter violently attacked and disfigured Malchus.

It was a shocking and confusing moment. Malchus was wounded and Peter stood over him, threatening another blow. The soldiers drew their weapons, ready to rush in and rescue their wounded compatriot. Suddenly Jesus demanded "No more of this!" There were too many victims already.

Even our victimizers are victims. It's just hard to see or care.

6. Forgive to Bring Healing

Those who victimize others suffer self-inflicted wounds. They diminish and damage themselves and inevitably suffer because of their actions. But the truth remains: the power to set things right is in the hands of their victim.

That's not the way most people see it. They think the power to heal is in the hands of the victimizer. Those people should make amends, suffer for their crimes, or at least apologize. To suggest that victims are somehow more powerful than their victimizers defies everyday logic. But that is exactly what Jesus shows.

Peter was in no mood to help Malchus, and even if he wanted to he couldn't. People can apologize, make restitution, suffer grievously for their wrongs, but their victims remain maimed. No amount of amends sets things right. That's not to say it doesn't matter. It does. It's healing for the victimizers to own their wrongs and do all in their power to set things right. But it doesn't automatically heal their victims.

Forgiveness heals both. The victimizer is freed from the debt and the victim is freed from collecting that debt. Both are freed from the past and able to embrace the future. Restoration and reconciliation become possible.

That power is in the hands of the victim—but not the victim alone. Anyone standing there that night could have reached out to help Malchus. Maybe some tried. But none of them had the power to heal him. Only God could do that. We can comfort those in pain and be comforted in our pain. Such acts are magnificent and healing in and of themselves—no divinity required. But the miracle Malchus needed, and what so many long for, is beyond human ability. Fortunately for Malchus, Jesus was divine. Fortunately for all of us he still is.

7. Surrender

Jesus told Peter, "Put your sword away! Am I not to drink the cup the Father has given me?" (John 18:11)

Jesus surrendered to God and God's will, not to the temple guards.

Some fights aren't worth having. If Jesus fought back that night the outcome wasn't in question; he'd win. Instead Christ let his enemies lead him away. Sometimes the road to real victory is surrender. But how do you know when to fight and when to surrender?

When you have to betray who you are and what you believe to win, it isn't worth it.

When you have to sacrifice the future to win today, it isn't worth it.

When winning only sets up the next battle, it isn't worth it.

When the only way to win is to destroy someone else, it isn't worth it.

In the end we too need to surrender to God's will and way and trust his work and his ultimate justice in our lives.

The parable of the prodigal son (Luke 15:11-32) has two responses to one great injury. In demanding his inheritance the younger brother dishonored his father and abandoned his responsibilities and his brother to pursue his own selfish desires. But the father didn't resist. He surrendered to the boy's demands. At the end of the day the father got what mattered most: his boy came home. The father, a victim, held the key to healing restoration and victory by not fighting.

The older brother didn't see it that way. He was angered by his father's forgiveness and generosity and refused to join the victory celebration. He complained about the way he was treated. Righteously indignant and embittered, he retaliated and lost what mattered most: his brother, his father, and the joy he could have shared.

So much for fighting back.

Easter is the story of our wounded healer. Jesus knows pain and suffering firsthand. Easter belongs to the wounded and suffering. In his presence they meet the God who loved them so much he willingly endured agony to win their eternity. He came to heal the wounds we suffer and forgive the wounds we inflict on others. The glory and triumph of Easter is that Christ joins us in our misery to comfort and restore. He is with us, a fellow sufferer who reaches out to touch our broken lives and heal us, just as he did Malchus.

Who'll Stop the Rain?

Ipulled in behind the last car in the funeral cortege. The defroster cleared the windows and the windshield wipers worked overtime but still couldn't keep up with the rain.

I hated conducting funerals of children and dreaded the graveside service. The young mother had given birth to twin boys. One died within hours and the other clung to the slimmest thread of life in a distant hospital's neonatal unit. If that weren't enough, the family would bury their little one in a driving rain.

Most church people don't believe it but it's true: pastors deal with people at the very worst moments of their lives and see so much misery and pain that sometimes it is hard to keep believing in a God of love, mercy, and compassion. Sometimes he seems to stand on the sidelines and let the sewer of human suffering overflow.

The longer I drove the angrier I got. I found myself railing at a God who would let a child die and then make this grieving family bury him in a drenching rain. Where was the caring God I preached, taught, and believed in? Their suffering seemed to matter more to me than it did to him. I pounded the steering wheel and let the anger out.

After a few minutes my rant turned into a simple prayer. "Please, God, don't make them bury their baby in the rain."

I didn't notice it at first, but the longer I drove the more the rain slowed. Soon it was just a sprinkle. The rain stopped by the time I turned into the country cemetery's dirt driveway. I parked out of the way. The family waited for me at the back of the hearse. I got out of the car and looked up at the dark, roiling, and ominous sky. The air was thick and heavy. But it wasn't raining.

I took my Bible but left the umbrella.

I led the procession up the dirt road to the grave near the top of a small hill and watched as the young father placed the tiny white coffin on the small bier surrounded by artificial grass that hid the grave and the mound of dirt and sod.

I waited for the family to gather and began the brief service.

When it was over I stood silently at the foot of the coffin and watched the family make their way down the hill to their cars, pull out of the cemetery, and head for the church and the funeral dinner. Two men got out of a truck parked inconspicuously at the edge of the cemetery, reached into the pick-up's bed, and pulled out shovels. They were there to finish the job. They pulled back the artificial grass, carefully lowered the coffin into the grave, removed the bier, and put the lid on the vault. They quickly filled the grave, did their best to reposition the sod, and made sure the small grave marker was in place. They rubbed the excess dirt from the blades of their shovels in the wet grass, threw them in the back of the truck, and drove away.

That's when the first heavy drop of rain fell. I walked as quickly as I could to the car. Running on a slick, rain-soaked dirt road wasn't a good idea. By the time I reached the car I was soaked to the skin. I could not remember ever seeing rain fall so hard so fast.

I sat in the car listening to the rain drum on the roof.

"Okay, I get it," I said quietly, reverently.

I did get it. I learned a lesson I'll never forget. There is a God who sees and cares, a God who noticed one grieving family in a small country cemetery—the same God who stilled the Sea of Galilee and healed his attacker in the garden—and opened the floodgates of heaven that day to make a point. It was the God who heard one of his doubting children ask him to stop the rain.

Chapter 3

When Worlds Collide

Reminiscere

2nd Sunday in Lent

Introit
Reminiscere miserationum tuarum Domine
Remember, O Lord.
Psalm 25:6 (KJV)

Remember, O LORD, thy tender mercies and thy lovingkindnesses;
for they have been ever of old.
Remember not the sins of my youth, nor my transgressions:
according to thy mercy remember thou me
for thy goodness' sake, O LORD.
Psalm 25:6-7 (KJV)

As soon as we are alone . . . inner chaos opens up.
—Henri J. M. Nouwen

The Voyage Home

The centurion was halfway through a delicious dinner, a very good wine, and a delightful conversation with the ship's captain when one of his men knocked on the door.

"This better be important," the old soldier warned.

"Sir, it's one of the prisoners. He said he knows you and asked to talk to you."

"You interrupted my dinner for that?" The old soldier's voice crackled with anger.

"No sir."

"Then what?"

"He said you've been looking for something and he knows where you can find it. I told him he was crazy . . . that I wouldn't bother you with that. Then he said to tell you, 'The dead come back to life,'" said the puzzled young soldier.

Instantly images of a long-ago crucifixion flooded the centurion's mind. "Take him to my quarters. I'll be there in a few minutes."

He finished the wine, thanked the captain, and went to his quarters. When he got there the prisoner waited calmly. He was small and balding. His beard and hair were gray and his eyes were tired.

"I am Julius, centurion of the Augustan cohort," announced the old soldier.

"I am Paul, an apostle of Jesus Christ. The man you crucified."

It all flooded back. The execution of this teacher was unlike anything he ever experienced. The events of those few days had shaken him to the core.

He'd been there when they arrested that Jew and ready for a fight when one of his followers attacked a temple guard. The teacher touched the

43

wounded man and healed his ear as if it had never happened; at least that's what he thought he saw. He knew the temple guard, but he couldn't remember his name. It bothered him.

They took the teacher to the Jewish council, then to Pilate, then to Herod and back to Pilate. His most skilled soldier scourged the prisoner within an inch of his life. The old soldier had laughed and jeered when his men braided a crown of thorns and jammed it on his head, draped an old robe over his shoulders, and paraded him in front of the crowd proclaiming him "King of the Jews."

He'd led the procession from the Fortress Antonia to Golgotha and made sure the beating, walk to the cross, and execution were carried out with great professionalism and skill. He saw it again and again in his nightmares; the procedure was always the same.

The two thieves cursed but the teacher carried his cross without complaint until he collapsed and a bystander was forced to pick it up for him.

When they crucified him the teacher didn't curse the Romans or rail against the crowd. While the soldiers gambled for his robe, the Rabbi made sure his mother was cared for and asked his God to forgive his executioners.

"Father, forgive them; for they do not know what they are doing."
(Luke 23:34)

It made no sense. Of course the Jews knew what they were doing. They plotted, planned, manipulated Pilate and perverted their own law to see this man crucified. No. He meant something else. The centurion couldn't figure it out. It bothered him.

When the teacher died the sky grew dark and the earth shook. The soldier heard himself saying, "This man was truly innocent—the Son of God." He remembered the shocked look on his soldiers' faces when they heard him. But deep in the center of his being, the centurion knew it was true.

Just as quickly, though, he'd put it aside. He did his job.

He personally pushed Pilate's insignia into wax to seal the tomb. The Jews put a guard on the tomb to make sure his disciples didn't steal the body. A few days later rumors that the man had come back from the dead filled Jerusalem.

Of course he didn't believe it.

He pulled aside the temple guards to get the real story. They hadn't fallen asleep. His disciples didn't steal the body. The guards were paid to lie. The rest of their story was just too fantastic to believe.

Then the movement started. Men and women declared that the teacher was alive. Thousands believed in him. It spread like wildfire. The Jewish leaders went after them with a vengeance. Ultimately the story spread to other parts of the empire and people who weren't Jews believed. Everywhere his followers went, they brought a quiet revolution that shook the foundations of Roman civilization.

"Now I remember you," the centurion told the old man before him. "But you weren't one of his followers. What was it they called you? Oh yes, 'the terror of Tarsus.' You worked for the Jewish religious leaders, the uh, uh. . . ."

"The Sanhedrin," said the prisoner.

"Yes, the Sanhedrin. You were their exterminator-in-chief. You had one of them stoned. I can't remember his name."

"Stephen."

"Yes, Stephen. Pilate didn't want trouble with the Jews so you got away with it."

"That's right," said Paul. "But I didn't really get away with anything."

"So what are you doing here?" asked the soldier.

"It's a long story. I'm one of Jesus's followers now. I took his message throughout Asia Minor and Greece. They arrested me. I defended myself before Felix and, two years later, before Festus and Agrippa. I'm a Roman citizen, so I appealed to Caesar."

The two old men stared at each other in silence. Finally the centurion spoke. "You said I was looking for something."

"That's right," answered Paul.

"Well, what is it?" the centurion asked with a smirk.

"You're looking for an answer that will bring you peace."

It took every ounce of control the old soldier could muster to maintain his stoic exterior. He had not had a moment's peace since that day. His declaration that the man on the center cross was the Son of God was at odds with everything he believed and valued. But it was true.

"How do you know that?" he asked.

"My God told me."

"So if it's true—and I'm not saying it is—where can I find what I'm looking for?"

"Where you lost it—at his feet. You can't live in two worlds, my friend. Either Jesus is the true, divine Lord or Nero is. You'll never have peace until you give yourself to what you know is true. You saw it the day he died. I saw it on the way to arrest his followers in Damascus."

The old soldier sat on the edge of his bunk, rested his elbows on his knees, his face in his hands, and absentmindedly stroked his chin and rubbed his eyes. The old Jew was right. He'd spent long years trying to escape what happened that day and the truth he could not deny.

"So . . . what do I have to do?" His voice betrayed what he would not let his face show.

"Simple, repent and believe. He's your Savior and my Messiah. He's Lord, not Nero."

"I'll think about it," said the centurion.

"Haven't you thought about it long enough?" asked the prisoner.

"It plagues me, that's true. By the end of this voyage I'll decide. We'll talk again."

"Of course, centurion. I'm at your disposal—literally," Paul said with a slight smile and nod as he rubbed his wrists left raw by the shackles. "One more thing, sir."

"What?"

"About waiting. Before our voyage ends, the cargo and the ship will be lost and our lives will be at great risk," warned the apostle.

"How do you know that?" the centurion asked.

The prisoner smiled.

Julius, centurion of the Augustus cohort, the battle-scarred lion of the empire, sent the prisoner back to his cell. Wine and weariness overwhelmed him. His valet helped him out of his armor and took it to be cleaned and polished. He stretched out on the bunk. The ship rolled gently in the waves and he drifted into a deep, dreamless sleep.

The Centurion at the Cross

Matthew 27:54; Mark 15:39; Luke 23:47

A war rages in the depths of every soul. Most find only an uneasy armistice. A voice that can be stilled but never silenced cries from beneath the surface. We search for a truth that is forever near but seems always out of reach. We are at war when a truth we cannot deny confronts the lives we live.

> When the centurion and those with him who were guarding Jesus saw the earthquake and what had just happened, they were filled with awe and said, "This was certainly God's Son." (Matthew 27:54)

On Golgotha the centurion watched an innocent man die with dignity, courage, and honor. To the jeering crowd, the Roman soldiers gambling for his robes and the centurion, this man offered forgiveness:

> Jesus said, "Father, forgive them, for they don't know what they're doing."(Luke 23:34)

To the miserable, dying criminal he offered hope:

> Jesus replied, "I assure you that today you will be with me in paradise." (Luke 23:43)

To his grieving friends and family he offered selfless love and a future:

> He said to his mother, "Woman, here is your son." Then he said to the disciple, "Here is your mother." (John 19:26-27)

To God he offered the truth of his tortured soul:

"My God, my God, why have you left me?" (Mark 15:34)

To his tormentors he offered the honest agony of a dying man:

"I am thirsty." (John 19:28)

To a world that did not understand he declared victory in the great work of human redemption:

"It is completed." (John 19:30)

To all who listen he gave the greatest example of a living and magnificent faith:

"Father, into your hands I entrust my life." (Luke 23:46)

The Crucifixion and the Centurion

The Romans made sure everyone knew who ruled. It wasn't that drunken popinjay Herod or the graybeards in the Sanhedrin. Pilate's soldiers patrolled Jerusalem's streets to demonstrate Rome's absolute power and intimidate a restless population. Crucifixion wasn't unusual and was always very public. That was the point. Crucifixion sent a crystal clear message: challenge us, disobey us, rebel against us, break our laws, and this is what you'll get.

But when Christ's head sagged in death, the centurion declared what was beyond dispute:

> When the centurion saw what happened, he praised God, saying,
> "It's really true: this man was righteous." (Luke 23:47)

The centurion heard it all and saw it all. He felt the earth quake below his feet and saw the sky turn from morning blue to midnight black. He was an irrefutable witness to the greatest single event in human history and had no reason to lie. He was not a sympathetic follower of Jesus or his Jewish tormentors, didn't believe their God, keep their customs, or have any reason other than what he saw and heard. Yet he made one of history's truly amazing statements.

The story of this unnamed Roman echoes through the Gospel accounts. His life was forever intertwined with Christ's the moment the Jews brought Jesus to Pilate and into Roman jurisdiction. We don't know his name, where he came from, how long he'd been in Palestine, or a hundred other details. All of that is lost in history.

Some believe he is St. Longinus. According to the legend, Longinus was transformed by the death and resurrection of Christ. He left the legion, joined the apostles, and preached in Cappadocia. There he was arrested, tortured, and ultimately beheaded for his faith. Like many traditions, the story of St. Longinus may have some basis in fact. We don't know.

But, whether the legend is true or not, at one critical moment everything this Roman centurion knew and believed crashed into an unbelievable and undeniable fact:

> When the centurion, who stood facing Jesus, saw how he died, he said, "This man was certainly God's Son." (Mark 15:39)

When Worlds Collide

This dying teacher from another people and another religion who taught another truth challenged the centurion's ordered life. These two worlds could not coexist. He could not embrace Caesar as divine and this dying Rabbi as the Son of God. He could not defend the honor of Rome and the superiority of his culture in the face of this gross miscarriage of justice. He could not worship the pantheon of deities and embrace this man's God. He could not rely on the power of Rome in the face of a power that could block out the sun, shake the earth, and bring the dead back to life. Only one of those worlds could survive as the center of his life.

No one knows what happened to the centurion after that day. Perhaps he went back to the barracks, drank until the images of that day drowned in the dark wine and sleep came, got up the next day, and went back to work.

But on Golgotha the centurion saw a world beyond his reality. That moment challenged each of the seven diligently defended "truths" on which people still build life, "truths" that cannot survive a confrontation with the truth.

1. Power

Power is the ability to influence the world and can be used for great good or great evil.

The centurion was an agent of the most powerful political and military empire the planet had ever seen. He wielded life and death in battle and in his authority over his soldiers. For hundreds of years the legions enforced Rome's will on the entire known world.

But that day the centurion confronted an undeniable power that did not rely on force, could not betray those who trusted it, and was greatest at the moment of surrender. Compared to that power, the mighty Roman Empire and her legions were children at play (John 19:8-11).

We learn early to cooperate with and rely on those who are more powerful. The young children depend on their parents to feed, clothe, and shelter them. We find security in our loyalty to our nation, our community or religion, or in those we love and who love us. Our security is in our allegiance to a company or a profession. We all navigate the dangerous shoals of power. Sometimes we use our power to further our ends. At other times we surrender to the powerful knowing that they can help us if we do and hurt us if we don't. That's reality.

There is another greater power. We cannot serve both but we will serve one (Philippians 2:5-8). Believers are not Pollyannaish. The powers we encounter in this life are very real. But there is a higher, greater, nobler power that permits the existence of lesser powers and has ultimate control. There are consequences for resisting political, economic, or personal power and physical force. But we need not fear anything or anyone if we rest fully in the power of God. Nothing is more powerful than his love (Romans 8:38-39).

2. People

People shape our world from the moment of birth. They interpret and explain our experiences and build the scaffolding of the truth we learn. Every encounter with the world is processed through the voice and touch of another person. The truth most believe is a human creation.

When family, clan, or culture collides with an incompatible reality we must choose between those worlds. On one side is everything we've been taught and everyone we know and love. On the other side are claims that cannot be denied but cannot be accepted without sacrifice. Embracing that new world means letting go of the only world we've ever known.

People matter to God, but people don't matter more than God. When these worlds collide some go with us; some don't. It is an inevitable consequence of seeing and pursuing another world (Matthew 19:27-30). Losing treasured relationships hurts. Nothing fills that void. But we find new, rich, and loving relationships in the company of the faithful and experience a love that surpasses anything human.

3. Passions

Our passions, the deep emotional bonds that hold the soil of our world in place, prevent the erosion of our worldview, filter what we can or cannot see, and forge our truth. It may be a lifestyle, a religion, or practices and rituals that bring us comfort and joy. Pleasure, wealth, property, and possessions can be at the core of one's passions. Others care deeply about their sense of pride or honor, political ideals, and social or personal values.

Conflicting passions ran white-hot on Golgotha. The Jews were passionate about preserving their place and willing to let an innocent man die. Jesus's followers were passionate about him and the future they thought he would create. The Romans cared about maintaining their power and control over a troubled province and a troublesome people.

But no one was prepared for the raw passion that flowed from the cross. Tortured, bleeding, and slowly dying, Jesus demonstrated a love unmatched in human history. He suffered an excruciating death to change the destiny of humankind. Such magnificent love was beyond the comprehension of those who plotted his murder, those who carried out the crime, and those who agonized with him.

Believers are not more or less passionate than anyone else. But they may be passionate about different things. Comfort, pleasure, power, possessions, influence, and status don't hold the allure for them (Matthew 22:36-40; John 13:34-35). Love God, love each other, love people: these are the touchstones of Christian passion.

4. The Past

The past is the bedrock of the present and future. Layer upon layer, the sediments of understanding and reality are laid down and passed on. New experiences are interpreted by the old and woven into the pattern of truth we learned in our mother's arms. The joy and pain, pleasures and sorrows, accomplishments and disappointments of our lives add nuance and texture to that tapestry.

The past matters. We all come with failure, transgressions, and trauma. But all of that passes away in Christ. It exists as a fact but no longer determines life or identity. The past that matters is not how we failed but what Christ did for us; not who we were but who we can be. Life is divided into the life we knew before Christ and the hope we know in Christ (2 Corinthians 5:17-18; Isaiah 64:8; Psalm 103:11-13).

5. Place

We all need a place to belong. Our place in the world may be defined by our name, our gender, our race, and the place and time of our birth. We grow up with parents, teachers, and neighbors telling us who we are, what we can and cannot do, and where we belong. Some find these confines restrictive. Most live comfortably within them and define themselves by them.

The Jews knew their place. The Roman centurion and his men knew where they belonged. Christ's followers thought they knew their place. But Jesus didn't play by the rules, refused to fit in, and would not submit to the religious and political authorities of the day. Jesus rejected the neat categories of his time, culture, and religion. He insisted on being who he was, the incarnate Son of God. They killed him for it.

Following Christ means leaving the safe confines. Jesus warned his followers what would happen if they did (Matthew 10:34-38). His followers are ostracized; they sometimes lose jobs, financial security, citizenship, and even their lives for his sake. It has always been true, is true today, and will be true until Christ's return.

But we find our true place in our relationship to him and to each other. We are interrelated and interdependent parts of the same building and members of the same body. We are valued by, belong to, and need each other. Each one is essential to life and the cause of Christ (1 Corinthians 3:9-11; 12:12-14; Ephesians 4:15-16).

6. Personal Identity

We can't know how the centurion saw himself. His service to Rome, his loyalty to the legion, and his men defined his position. Certainly he did not identify with a Jewish Rabbi who claimed to fulfill ancient prophecies. On display that crucifixion day was a radically different example of what it meant to be a man of integrity, honor, and courage. No one has seen anything like it before or since. It challenged the centurion.

Christ transforms us. We are no longer the products of our past, our circumstances, or our choices. We are freed to become what we were always meant to be and to find and fulfill our true identity (John 3:1-7). We experience a new sense of self on the road to fulfilling our God-given destiny. Freed from those limitations, we boldly step into an unimaginable future with a new identity. We are truly born again and made into new creations.

7. Prospects for the Future

Everyone imagines his or her prospects and dreams of a cherished future. The future is the destination of life's journey. Many long for a future defined by comfort, financial security, or a life of ease. Fame, notoriety, status, power, and position are in the futures others crave.

In crucifying Jesus, the Jewish leaders looked to the future believing they had secured peaceful coexistence with the Romans and their own power and influence. The Romans believed that they had avoided war and mollified a restless population. Christ's followers saw a bleak and foreboding future. Their hopes of reigning in his messianic kingdom were ground to dust.

None of them saw the future from the cross.

Sin and death had been defeated. The future was bright. The great exchange of man's sin for God's grace had been flawlessly completed and a new era dawned. Salvation had come: untold millions would experience God's love and forgiveness and know the joys of God's grace. Christ's victory was final, but his death was not. He would rise again and his church would spread that joy around the world.

No one on Golgotha that day got the future they expected except Jesus.

For most, the future is limited by life span. But the future for those who believe in Jesus is unbounded by time or space. We are immortal. That changes everything. Some choices make sense if the only future we can know is here and now. Other choices are sane only if we are immortal. Sacrifice, suffering, and self-denial become the wisest possible ways to live because they reap an everlasting reward.

In that future our prospects are certain. The Creator of the universe guarantees it! His plans are perfect, his power is infinite, and he executes his will flawlessly. He has promised a future in his presence and guaranteed a life without the pain, sorrow, and sin that plague us in this world. That is our forever.

War of the Worlds

Two worlds vie for everyone's heart, mind, and soul. One is the world we see, hear, touch, smell, and taste. Most live and die in and for that world.

The other world, the world of the Spirit, is just as real. But it is not necessarily the world of religion, even the Christian religion. Many religious people are firmly planted in the physical realm trying to gain favor with the divine by their righteous lives and religious practices—their own efforts.

People who truly encounter the realm of the Spirit begin to know God and his grace, love, and forgiveness. His work, not ours, matters. He accomplished what we can never do. No wonder these worlds collide.

For a very brief moment the centurion peered into the other world. Then he disappeared. Perhaps he dismissed what he saw and went on with life. Most prefer the certainty of a world they can see to one taken on faith. Others hope his story ended differently. I do. Perhaps that glimpse of glory turned him in a new direction and sent him searching for a greater truth. We'll know only in heaven.

In every life there is a moment when worlds collide. We catch a glimpse of glory and can choose to leave what we know and to live in a very different reality.

Some do. Most don't.

At Easter, Christ conquered the destructive, dissonant, and destructive forces that plague our broken world. He came to still our restless and troubled souls and fill our lives with the serenity of his certain love. He is not at war with us. We—like the centurion—are at war with him and with a truth we cannot deny. He does not come to threaten, bully, or demand. He does not come to criticize, demean, or point out our failures. He comes to forgive, to comfort, and to bring us peace. His followers become ambassadors bringing his message of relief and rest to suffering people and our shattered world. At Easter Christ reconciled our troubled lives and wandering souls to God who welcomes us home—if we will let him be our Prince of Peace.

VJ Day, 1990

April 8—Palm Sunday
April 13—Good Friday
April 15—Easter Sunday

They met on Easter Sunday when Jack visited church with his daughter. Now the old soldier and the young preacher sat in a corner of the hospital's empty family waiting room and talked quietly. Jack said he needed the walk and didn't want to talk in front of his roommate.

"How are you, Jack?"

"Feeling better. They say I can go home tomorrow and back to work next week if I feel up to it," said Jack.

"That's great. Glad to hear it! I'm a little surprised you asked to talk with me. Hasn't Father Bill been around to see you?" the preacher asked.

"He's been here. He's okay for a priest. But I wanted to talk to someone else. You don't mind, do you?"

"No, of course not."

"Do you know what day it is?" the old soldier asked.

The young preacher wasn't sure how to answer but decided to try a little humor.

"Sure, it's Tuesday, September 2. But I don't think that's what you had in mind, is it?"

"It's VJ Day. You know, the day the Japanese surrendered in Tokyo harbor and the war in the Pacific ended," the old soldier said.

"Did you serve in the Pacific, Jack?"

"Yes. I was seventeen when I joined the Marines and ended up in some pretty awful places. I did some awful things. I haven't talked about it with any-body, not Nell, not my kids, not even a priest."

"Is that what you want to talk about?"

The old man paused to gather his thoughts, took a deep breath, and told his story.

Fighting across a Pacific island Jack and his squad were pinned down by accurate and deadly sniper fire. The Marines did not return fire, fearing their muzzle flashes would give away their exact positions. His sergeant ordered Jack and two other Marines to work their way behind the snipers and take them out silently.

They did exactly that. Each man crawled alone into the jungle. Peering through the underbrush Jack spotted a lone Japanese soldier crouched behind a fallen log pointing his rifle in the direction of Jack's squad. Inching closer Jack waited, then burst from hiding and attacked the sniper. Each man was determined to kill the other. In the end Jack wrestled his enemy to the ground and strangled him to death with his bare hands. When it was over Jack rifled through the man's pockets and pack looking for maps, orders, or anything of military value.

Jack found a letter that had been opened, read, carefully refolded, and returned to its envelope many times. Tucked inside the envelope was a pho-tograph of a beautiful young Japanese woman holding a small child. She was a widow and her child was orphaned at his hand. The man whose lifeless eyes stared at a cloudless sky wasn't just the enemy. He was a much-loved son, hus-band, and father. And Jack found a crucifix.

Jack's squad moved forward and found him sitting next to the dead sol-dier, staring at the picture and holding the crucifix. He was rotated to the rear for some rest and the war ended before they sent him back to his unit.

That's when the nightmares began.

He started to drink so he could sleep. Then he drank to get through the day. Finally, he just drank.

The old soldier paused, wiped the tears from his cheeks, and blew his nose into a wad of tissue pulled from the pocket of his hospital robe.

"I don't think God can forgive me for what I did that day."

The two men sat in silence for a long time.

"I can't say I understand, Jack. I never served in the military. But I think the guilt you feel means you're a good man who understands that you had to do something terrible. It means you're a compassionate man who can feel for another person's suffering. Frankly it would worry me more if you didn't regret what happened that day.

"But you said you don't think God can forgive you for what you did that day. You're wrong, Jack. He can. He will."

The preacher pulled the small New Testament he always carried on hospital visits from his jacket pocket, opened it to Luke 23, and read:

> One of the criminals hanging next to Jesus insulted him: "Aren't you the Christ? Save yourself and us!" Responding, the other criminal spoke harshly to him, "Don't you fear God, seeing that you've also been sentenced to die? We are rightly condemned, for we are receiving the appropriate sentence for what we did. But this man has done nothing wrong." Then he said, "Jesus, remember me when you come into your kingdom." (Luke 23:39-42)

"Jack, if Jesus could forgive the people who tortured and crucified him, if he could welcome the thief on the cross into heaven, he can forgive you—if you let him. That's not the problem. Jack, can you forgive yourself?"

The young preacher and the old soldier talked a long time that afternoon and prayed together before Jack went back to his room. Jack slept deeply and peacefully that night. He did not dream.

Chapter 4

On the Road to Discovery

Oculi

3rd Sunday in Lent

Introit
Oculi mei simper ad Dominum.
Mine eyes are ever toward the Lord.
Psalm 25:15a

Mine eyes are ever toward the Lord;
for he shall pluck my feet out of the net.
Turn thee unto me, and have mercy upon me;
for I am desolate and afflicted.
Psalm 25:15-16 (KJV)

Men go abroad to wonder at the heights of mountains, at the huge waves of
the sea, at the long courses of the rivers, at the vast compass of the ocean, at the
circular motions of the stars, and they pass by themselves without wondering.
—St. Augustine of Hippo

Road Trip

Note: One of the men on the Road to Emmaus is identified as Cleopas (Luke 24:18). Tradition holds that he was also known as Alpheus, the father of James the Less and the younger brother of Joseph, Mary's husband and Christ's stepfather.

"Tell me about your nephew."

"He wasn't my nephew."

They sat across from each other under the shade of an awning. The writer explained his assignment, brought greetings from mutual friends, and tried to build rapport with the old man. It didn't work. He decided to try again.

"Well, tell me about your brother's oldest son then."

"He wasn't my brother's son."

"I know, but there must have been a time when you thought of him as your nephew."

"No. Never did."

"But your brother adopted him and claimed him as his own. People thought of him as his oldest boy, right?"

"Wrong. Everybody knew the truth."

"What was he like when he was growing up?"

"Not much to tell," the old man responded.

The writer waited, thinking the silence was a pregnant pause before some great revelation.

Wrong again. The old man had said all he was going to say.

Getting the old man to talk was proving a lot harder than the writer thought it would be.

Time to change tactics, he thought.

"Can I ask you about something that happened after he died?"

"You mean after they tortured and murdered him?" The old man barely masked his rage.

"Yes, after they murdered him. Will you tell me about it?"

"You mean what happened on the road?"

"Yes."

The young writer waited until the old man began to talk.

"After he died we stayed in the city for a few days.

"My Mary and the other women wanted to comfort his mother. His followers were in hiding, afraid the authorities would come after them and their families. I decided to leave the city and headed out with a good friend who lived about seven miles away, in Emmaus. On the way we met a young man who walked along with us. He said we looked sad and asked what we were talking about.

"So I asked him if he was the only one in the city who didn't know the things that had happened.

"He asked, 'What things?'

"So we talked all the way to Emmaus about the crucifixion.

"When we got near the village we thought he was going farther. We urged him to stay with us. When we sat down to eat, my friend asked the stranger to pray. He took the bread, blessed and broke it, and gave it to us. That's when it happened. I don't know why I didn't recognize him before. But when he broke the bread and prayed I knew it was Mary's boy! He was alive! Then he was gone. He just vanished!

"Sounds crazy, doesn't it?" the old man asked.

"Not to me. I've seen some pretty crazy things myself. What happened then?"

"My friend and I talked about all he told us on the road and how he explained the scriptures and decided we had to go back. We left right away, went back to the city, found some of his closest followers, and told them everything that happened. They told us that Mary's boy had appeared to Peter and the others but they didn't believe that we'd seen him too."

"It must have been incredible," the writer replied.

"It was, it really was." The old man had a faraway look in his eye. "You believe me?"

"Yes I do. Thanks for telling me."

"You're welcome. By the way, what's your name? If you told me I'm sorry. I forgot."

"Luke. My name is Luke."

Cleopas

Luke 24:13-35; Mark 16:12-13

No one knows why Cleopas and his companion were on their way to Emmaus. But we know they weren't expecting to encounter the resurrected Christ. They weren't just on the road to Emmaus; they were on the road to a stunning discovery.

Every life is a journey to discover who we are, why we are here, and what matters most. We want to discover our own way rather than follow the ways of family, friends, community, or peers. We want to find ourselves: it's a very odd statement. But it's one of the most common human experiences.

But what are we trying to discover? What do we want to know? Are we looking for peace, love, well-being, belonging, satisfaction, achievement, happiness, or some other internal sense? Are we looking for one thing or is it a mosaic? Are we putting together the jigsaw puzzle of our lives until our true image emerges?

Like the road to Emmaus, the road to discovery falls into three distinct segments: roadblocks, steps, and signposts.

Roadblocks to Discovery

If Cleopas was Christ's uncle as some think, it's remarkable that he and his companion did not recognize Jesus. He was close enough to listen in as they talked, ask questions, and carry on a conversation. Jesus was with them and they didn't realize it. The question is why?

> On that same day, two disciples were traveling to a village called Emmaus, about seven miles from Jerusalem. They were talking to each other about everything that had happened. While they were discussing these things, Jesus himself arrived and joined them on their journey. They were prevented from recognizing him. (Luke 24:13-16)

Distractions

The men were preoccupied with getting away from Jerusalem and the events of the previous days.

We too are on our way from wherever we are to where we think we are going. Our minds, hearts, and passions are engaged with that journey and we are distracted by its myriad details and challenges. These distractions keep us from seeing the God who is with us.

Preconceptions

Jesus no longer fit their preconceived notions. The Messiah was to be a conquering king, not someone executed like a common criminal. They suffered from paradigm blindness. Jesus was near enough to touch but he wasn't what they expected, and they couldn't see him.

Many never discover the truth they seek because they cannot see it. We are blinded to all other possibilities, including the miraculous, the spiritual, and the divine, by a paradigm that excludes any way of living other than what we already know. We can't see what we believe is impossible. If we believe that happiness, meaning, and fulfillment are not possible, they become impossible. Every great discovery begins with the belief that it is possible.

> He said to them, "What are you talking about as you walk along?"
> They stopped, their faces downcast. The one named Cleopas replied,
> "Are you the only visitor to Jerusalem who is unaware of the things
> that have taken place there over the last few days?"
> He said to them, "What things?" They said to him, "The things
> about Jesus of Nazareth." (Luke 24:17-19a)

Headed in the Wrong Direction

The companions' goal was a dusty little village seven miles away from the empty tomb. They missed the grandeur of the resurrection, the advent of the kingdom of God, and the inauguration of the church and its mission because they were looking somewhere else. Focused on what was in front of them, they could not see what was happening around them.

Some believe finding what their hearts most long for is impossible. It is a tragic self-fulfilling prophecy that bankrupts the soul. They never reach the goal, not because they can't but because they fail to factor in the Divine. It is always a grave mistake.

Steps on the Road to Discovery

Those unwilling to make the journey of discovery will never find what they seek.

A Journey

The two on the road to Emmaus were preoccupied, distracted, and headed in the wrong direction. They were blind to the magnificent encounter that awaited them. But they were moving in the direction of discovery. Those who seek are the only ones who find.

New Truth

Luke is very clear on this point: Cleopas and his companion thought they knew what the Old Testament said about the Messiah and it wasn't what happened on Golgotha. Christ's interpretation of the scriptures opened their eyes to the possibility of new discovery and corrected what they grossly misunderstood.

> Then Jesus said to them, "You foolish people! Your dull minds keep you from believing all that the prophets talked about. Wasn't it necessary for Christ to suffer these things and then enter into his glory?" (Luke 24:25-26)

Discovering a new life demands taking a hard look at what we think we know. The fact that most of the time, and for most people, traditional ways don't work doesn't stop people from following them or teaching them to others. Without new truth we are stuck in the well-worn ruts of our pasts. Many

71

reject what they think Christianity teaches. They are wrong. A divine encounter opens the door to rediscovering long-misunderstood ancient truths.

Partners

Jesus walked and stayed with the men. We rarely take the journey to discovery alone. Insights are personal, but the process of discovery happens in relationship with those who have already found it.

> While they were discussing these things, Jesus himself arrived and joined them on their journey. (Luke 24:15b)

True guides know the way and are honest seekers. They are patient. Truth dawns in each heart and mind on its own schedule. Guides invest in others. Of all the places Christ could have been at that moment he chose to invest in these two men.

Sadly, many follow false guides down dangerous and disastrous paths even when they know it's risky. It's a formula for disaster.

Encounter

> When they came to Emmaus, he acted as if he was going on ahead. But they urged him, saying, "Stay with us. It's nearly evening, and the day is almost over." So he went in to stay with them. After he took his seat at the table with them, he took the bread, blessed and broke it, and gave it to them. Their eyes were opened and they recognized him, but he disappeared from their sight. (Luke 24:28-31)

Some choose the inward path of self-reflection and self-examination rather than the path to a divine revelation. But the weight of biblical evidence is against them. The great figures of the Bible all came to know themselves and their purposes in encounters with God. We see clearest when we examine ourselves in the bright light of divine revelation, not the shadows of human insight.

Our ability to understand often exceeds our ability to act on that understanding. It may take time for our lifestyles to catch up with the truths we discover. But that doesn't mean the encounter is any less important. God doesn't always shout from heaven. Sometimes he whispers in the depths of the soul. That doesn't make it any less his voice.

Signposts of Discovery

After their encounter with Christ, Cleopas and his companion returned to Jerusalem to tell the disciples.

Mark's account makes it clear that the others didn't believe their story. It isn't surprising. Peter and John didn't believe Mary Magdalene and Thomas didn't believe the combined testimony of the other ten disciples.

> After that he appeared in a different form to two of them who were
> walking along in the countryside. When they returned, they reported
> it to the others, but they didn't believe them. (Mark 16:12-13)

Every person's path to his or her encounter with God is unique. The best route to discovery is always a firsthand experience. Others' experiences, no matter how real or how sincere, are exactly that—other persons' experiences. They may be entirely truthful and accurate. Cleopas and his companion were. But even if we believe them, the discovery doesn't impact us in the same way. How could it? Their story is a pale shadow, not the vivid and vibrant colors of personal experience.

> They said to each other, "Weren't our hearts on fire when he spoke
> to us along the road and when he explained the scriptures for us?"
> (Luke 24:32)

Discovery changes everything. A divine encounter transforms us at the deepest level.

But most of all it changes how we see ourselves. Doubters and skeptics become passionate believers and are radically transformed by that truth.

Discovery opens hearts and minds to new possibilities. Cleopas and his companion saw a profoundly different reality. They no longer lived in the strictures of their old lives. What had been impossible was suddenly and irrevocably possible and present.

Discovery sets life on a new course. Cleopas and his companion "immediately . . . went back to Jerusalem" (Luke 24:33). They had reached their destination. But encountering Christ sent them on an entirely new, unanticipated, and revolutionary journey.

In that change of direction we find our reason for being and we find ourselves. Most are headed away from, not toward, discovering life and purpose in God. Persisting in the wrong direction only carries us further and further from our goal. But charting a new course seems risky. A well-traveled path, even if it leads nowhere, seems safer than blazing a trail.

Discovery is not permanent. Jesus vanished once they recognized him. At that moment those two could have gone back to their original plan and let the strange encounter fade into the past. But they let the experience change them. It's tempting to settle back into the comfortable patterns of life after a powerful experience. But only those who act on what they discover truly change.

Undiscovered Lives

What does it mean to discover our truest identities and highest purposes?

There are certain bedrock assumptions to discovering true identity and purpose. First, all reality is God's creation. Our world is what God made it and we are who and what we are because he made us this way. Second, man is unique in all creation. We share certain characteristics with the other creatures in our world. Why would we expect anything else? We live in this world and our bodies must breathe air, drink water, deal with gravity, and do thousands of other things every bird, fish, insect, plant, or animal must do. But we alone bear the "image of God" (Genesis 1:26-27).

Finally, things are not as God intended. Something went terribly wrong. Humankind's fall from grace and expulsion from Eden is a tragic and disturbing story (Genesis 3). That moment damaged our nature and our relationships with God, his creation, and each other. Every generation compounds the problem by adding their rebellion and rejection of God's will and ways. We are a very long way from who and what our designer meant us to be.

As created beings we truly discover ourselves only when we meet the Creator and discover what he created us for and why. The Genesis account emphasizes three dimensions of every life—character, creativity, and community.

1. Character

We are made in God's image and with his character. Like God we are spirit and the human spirit survives physical death. We are immortal but not eternal; God alone is without beginning or end. We share attributes of God's character with every other person. But each person is a unique and divine creation (Psalm 139:13-14; Isaiah 64:8; Romans 9:19-24).

We were created for a single grand purpose: to know and love God. Each person has a unique reason for his or her life within that grand purpose. We find it in God's will, in his gifts, in his graces, and in our relationship with our Creator. We find joy, meaning, and purpose in singular ways. But all of it is a gift from God. We honor God when we use his gifts of creativity and community to add value to the world and to the lives of others, and to bring glory to him.

2. Creativity

We alone share God's ability to truly create. Creativity is not problem solving, intelligence, the ability to adapt, or the clever use of what we already know. Creativity is something completely different; it is the capacity to imagine what has never been and bring it into existence.

Many don't think of themselves as creative and don't pursue expression. Many accept the limited definitions of creativity from culture and society. Sometimes we value fitting in more than creativity and individuality. But every person longs to express his or her innate creative capacity and unique personhood.

3. Community

We were created for community. Only one thing wasn't good in all creation: being alone. So God created a companion for Adam. The intimacy of the Trinity is echoed in the relationship between the man, the woman, and God. We cannot be alienated from others and the God who loves us and still find ourselves.

Sharing value with others is not limited to marriage partners, family, friends, or even community. As wonderful as these things are, they cannot meet our deepest cravings. The only place we see our true reflection is by looking at God. He knows our worth. He knows what he created us for. He knows what fulfills our deepest needs. He knows our strengths and weaknesses. God alone can answer life's most profound question: Who am I?

People are both beautiful and broken. Created in the image of God, we turned our backs on him and his wisdom, will, and ways. We cannot know who we are until we know the one who created us and knew us before the beginning of time. We were brought into being to display his glory and reflect his likeness in the world. We know ourselves only when we find our place in this world and in his presence.

Cleopas and his companion found themselves in him, in his call, and in his great mission. They found what we all seek.

The cross stands at the center of every Easter celebration. It towers above history as a beacon to remind us that Christ came to help us find our way to him. We all follow a road that leads either to his cross or to a road that leads away from it. Easter belongs to the searchers, the wanderers, and the lost. It belongs to the failing and the faithful. Easter belongs to all who look up and follow the way of the cross despite their questions, doubts, and fears. Those who follow that road live in the company of Christ, who took the road to his cross for us.

The Hard Road, 1967

March 19—Palm Sunday
Mach 24—Good Friday
March 26—Easter Sunday

The family reunion was, well, a reunion of a family that had been scattered from its North Dakota beginnings to Washington State and Alaska, California, Idaho, Michigan, and Ohio for decades. Most of us had no clue who belonged to whom, had only a distant connection to each other, and wouldn't have guessed we were related.

Walking across the park I looked for a shady spot for my kids to eat their hot dogs and spotted a familiar face. It was my aunt Gladys. Growing up I had considered Uncle Russell and Aunt Gladys my favorites.

Russell and Gladys Kensinger went to Nicaragua in 1945 as missionaries. When they came home to visit supporting congregations, they often stayed with our family. Having Uncle Russell around was every boy's delight. He told tall tales of adventures in the jungle, had the longest snakeskin I'd ever seen, and revealed a collection of strange things from a faraway land. And he loved to tell stories.

When I was fourteen I overheard a conversation I wasn't supposed to hear. Uncle Russell had severe, life-threatening asthma. Doctors advised him to move to a warm, dry climate like Arizona or New Mexico and not return to sultry, damp Nicaragua. My parents tried to convince them to follow the doctors' advice.

Uncle Russell and Aunt Gladys listened quietly. I remember clearly how the conversation ended.

"What can we do? God has called us," said Uncle Russell.

Russell and Gladys went back to Nicaragua. Three months later Russell was dead. Aunt Gladys and their daughter settled in Washington State and we lived in Michigan. Trips to the West Coast were rare and other things got in the way. I hadn't seen her for almost twenty years.

"Hi, Aunt Gladys," I said.

It took a minute but a flicker of recognition crossed her face, then a bright smile, a warm hug, and a kiss on the cheek. I told her about my family, introduced my kids, and explained that I was a pastor. She told me about her daughter and grandchildren.

After a while I asked, "Do you stay in touch with people in Nicaragua?"

The floodgates opened and joy-filled stories of the people and places she had known and all the wonderful things that had happened poured out. She talked as if I knew them all. I didn't know any of them, but it didn't matter. I was swept up and carried along by her joy.

Gladys told me that during the last months of his life Russell connected with two young men. Both later played significant roles in the life of the church in Nicaragua. They were Russell's divine appointments and their lives and ministry were a lasting legacy to him, his love for God, Nicaragua, and its people.

One of my most painful childhood memories is the day my sister and I walked into the house a few weeks after Easter to find my mother weeping at the kitchen table. She looked up and simply said, "Uncle Russell is dead." That moment precipitated a deep crisis of faith. It took me years to come to terms with his death.

Twenty-two years after they went to Nicaragua we received this terse message via Western Union: "Russell . . . passed away . . . 3:15pm . . . Asthma . . . Buried Tuesday." It wasn't much of an epitaph. He'd chosen a hard road. But he made a long-term investment even when there was little or nothing to show for all that hard work and sacrifice.

But Uncle Russell saw the end of that road. He saw it all before it happened with the eyes of faith. And he saw it from heaven's shore.

Chapter 5

The Great Pretenders

Laetare

4th Sunday in Lent

Introit
Exultate iusti in Domino rectos decet laudation.
Psalm 33:1

Rejoice in the Lord, O ye righteous:
for praise is comely for the upright.
Praise the Lord with harp:
sing unto him with the psaltery and an instrument of ten strings.
Sing unto him a new song;
play skillfully with a loud noise.
Psalm 33:1-3 (KJV)

There are pretenders to piety as well as courage.
—Molière

The Trial

"I don't need to remind either of you how serious this is, do I?"

The three men sat around a small table talking quietly and no, they didn't need to be reminded. They knew exactly what would happen if they were convicted.

Nicodemus and Joseph of Arimathea would soon face the charges against them. The high priest would gather the members of the Great Sanhedrin in the Hall of Hewn Stone on the south side of the temple's great court. The members of the council would sit in a semicircle with the high priest in the center. Members of Jerusalem's two lesser councils, armed guards, and servants would be there to watch.

The accused would stand in the center with two advocates silently facing the high priest, dressed as if in mourning to demonstrate their humility and sorrow before the council. One advocate would register reasons for condemnation. The other would register reasons for acquittal. Then the council would vote.

The man with the questions would argue for their acquittal. He didn't relish this assignment. These two openly admitted that the accusations against them were true. He was as disgusted by them as the rest of the council. And he didn't want to face the brilliant prosecutor. He didn't like losing.

"What am I supposed to say to the council? 'Yes, they did everything you say they did, but they're nice guys so let them go'?"

The two defendants looked at each other and then at their frustrated advocate.

"No. No, we don't expect anything like that," said Joseph.

"We're accused of heresy, of believing in a false Messiah, and supporting those who preach in his name. Right?" asked Nicodemus.

"That's right," answered the advocate.

"Well, we're only guilty if he wasn't the Messiah, right?"

"Are you out of your minds?"

"But it's the truth," interjected Joseph.

"That's what you say. The high priest doesn't believe that. The council doesn't believe that. I don't believe it," answered the advocate. "Do I have to point out what happened to the last man who made that argument? Remember Stephen? They stoned him to death. In case you hadn't noticed, the prosecution advocate is the same man who instigated his stoning."

"You don't need to remind us," said Nicodemus. "He's Saul from Tarsus and a student of Gamaliel. He's ambitious and completely convinced he's doing the right thing."

"We knew Stephen too. He was a brave, good man who loved God," added Joseph.

"What he is is dead! That's what you're going to be if we don't figure out a defense that can win."

"Stephen is in heaven. Jesus taught us that we should not fear those who can kill the body, but rather God, who can destroy the soul," said Joseph.

"You've got a death wish, don't you? You want to be martyrs. I can't fight for you if you won't fight for yourself!"

Both men chuckled.

"No, we don't have a death wish."

"So what do you expect me to do?"

"Well, you could start by listening," said Nicodemus.

"All right, I'll listen."

"Why don't you start, Nicodemus? You believed in him before I did," said Joseph.

"Well, it started after I heard him speak to the crowd. I had questions but I was afraid to talk to him publicly, so I went to him at night. . . ."

For the next two hours Nicodemus and Joseph of Arimathea walked their advocate through their encounters with Jesus of Nazareth during the three years of his public ministry. They described his miracles, healings, and power over demonic forces. They explained his teachings and pointed out how Jesus fulfilled all the messianic prophecies. They reminded the advocate of the hundreds of eyewitnesses who had seen these things and how they became convinced that Jesus of Nazareth was the Messiah.

"I have a question," the advocate interrupted.

"Of course."

"So both of you believed in him before his crucifixion, right?"

"Yes."

"But you kept that a secret, didn't you?"

The two men looked at each other. It was clear the advocate had hit a nerve.

Finally, Nicodemus spoke up. "That's right. We were afraid—cowards. His disciples were brave enough to follow him in front of everyone until he was arrested. We weren't."

"We wanted to follow him. But we wanted to keep what we had—our power, wealth, positions, and the respect of others. So we pretended. But in the end we had to decide who we were," explained Joseph.

The advocate was intrigued. These rich, powerful men with so much to lose had, since Jesus's death, thrown it all away to follow a penniless, itinerant Rabbi and his rag-tag bunch of ignorant disciples. He knew he could never explain it to the council, but maybe the men could explain it to him.

"What happened? What changed?"

"They killed him," answered Joseph.

"We spoke against his arrest but we failed and they arrested, tortured, and executed him anyway. I'd told myself that if I kept my faith secret I could use my influence to protect him. I was wrong," said Nicodemus.

Joseph said, "After he was crucified I went to Pilate and asked for the body so we could bury him before the Sabbath. My servants brought spices and Nicodemus brought the shroud."

"We took him from the cross, cleaned him up as well as we could. We wanted to bury him with a little dignity. It was the least we could do," said Nicodemus.

"We took him to my new tomb in a garden not far from Golgotha," Joseph continued.

"When the women came back on the first day of the week to finish the burial preparations his body was gone—the tomb was open and empty. It still is," said Nicodemus.

"The women thought someone stole his body. Peter and John went to the tomb and couldn't find him either. That's when Mary from Magdala said she saw Jesus alive."

"Stop right there!" said the advocate. "You can't expect reasonable men to believe that story. It's outrageous! Crucified men don't come back from the dead. It's just a wild rumor started by emotional women and ignorant fishermen. The temple guards said his body was stolen while they slept."

The two men smiled at each other as if they shared some great secret.

"If those guards really fell asleep, would they be walking around today? You know death is the penalty for sleeping on duty," Joseph pointed out.

"We know he's alive. We saw him too. More than five hundred of us saw him the day he ascended into heaven. We all saw the same thing," added Nicodemus.

"Most of them are still in the city. You could talk to them," suggested Joseph.

"I don't want to talk to crazy people who think dead men wake up, walk out of their tombs, and then float into heaven!" Disdain filled the advocate's voice.

The three men fell silent as the advocate pondered his clients' story.

"So that's it? That's your defense? You're not guilty because Jesus of Nazareth really is the Messiah and the Son of God?"

"It's the truth."

"Well, that truth is going to get you stoned to death!"

Then it dawned on him. Men will die for a lie they believe is the truth. But men don't die for what they know is a lie. These two were in a position to know the truth. The council couldn't arrest and punish his followers fast enough. It just didn't make sense that so many were willing to lose so much for a lie.

He heard himself mutter, "They're telling the truth!" and felt the earth quake in his soul.

Nicodemus and Joseph of Arimathea

Matthew 27:57-61; Mark 15:42-47; Luke 23:50-56; John 19:38-42

"They don't belong to this world, just as I don't belong to this world."
(John 17:16)

These enigmatic and troubling words are from Christ's prayer in the garden. We are in the world but not of the world. What does that mean? Christ did not ask that his followers be taken from this world but be protected and sanctified in it. Somehow we belong and don't belong to this world—at the same time.

How is it possible to fully participate in life and not be "of the world"?

Some turn their backs on culture and society. Others contend believers can and should fully participate in all this world offers. Some, like Nicodemus and Joseph of Arimathea, lead double lives.

The Great Pretenders

Nicodemus and Joseph of Arimathea pretended to be what they were not. After his late-night encounter with Jesus, Nicodemus became a follower of Christ (John 3:1-5). Later he defended Jesus before the high priest and asked that the Sanhedrin follow its own rules and respect the rights of the accused. In the end they did neither and Nicodemus was ridiculed for his efforts (John 7:40-52). We don't know when Joseph of Arimathea crossed the line into faith.

During Christ's ministry both men went on with life as usual, continued to be part of the Jewish governing council, and never let on that they were followers of Christ.

As Christ gained prominence he went from being an amusing curiosity to being an annoyance and finally to being a danger to the religious and political status quo. In the end the Sanhedrin and its leadership determined to kill him. Tradition says Nicodemus spoke on Christ's behalf at his trial before Pilate. The Bible tells us that Joseph of Arimathea did not agree with the Sanhedrin's plan. After Christ's death, both took the very public step of attending to his body and his burial.

It's not surprising that these men kept their faith in Christ a secret. But it is amazing that they demonstrated the most courage precisely when they faced the greatest risk. It would have been far easier for them to confess Christ when he was a rising star and abandon him when things went bad. They did the opposite and chose the risky path of living authentic lives.

Unlikely Heroes

Nicodemus and Joseph of Arimathea were men with a lot to lose. They were rich, respected, and powerful and had climbed the ladder of success far enough to see the top rung. Their lives were built on and completely enmeshed with the power structures of the Sanhedrin, its politics, and its pharisaical religion. Their wives, children, and families benefited from their lives and depended on them. Openly following Christ would cost everything they had taken a lifetime to build (Luke 9:23-26).

It's no different today. Those open about their faith in Christ put themselves in harm's way. In some places a confession of faith means torture, prison, or martyrdom. In other places persecution means being overlooked for a promotion at work, losing a job, being denied admission to a school or university, or being rejected by family: disowned, divorced, or treated with great disdain.

Dissatisfied with the lives they led, these men looked for something better, the kingdom of God. They were honorable men who struggled with a very real dilemma. They were chameleons with a conscience. Living double lives bothered them.

Honorable people may fail to live up to their own standards but not without the pangs of conscience, and not for very long. The dissonance is too loud. They abandon the deception or are destroyed by it. Some give up on their standards and redefine themselves. Others watch their souls rot, unwilling to resolve the tension. Some play the charade, destroy their consciences, and are concerned only when they get caught.

For a while, Nicodemus and Joseph of Arimathea were men with a divisive secret. Believing in Christ would make them, in the eyes of their colleagues and culture, heretics who had abandoned their faith and national identity. In a few decades, what these two knew instinctively became obvious to all: one could be a Jew or a Christian. It wasn't what God wanted, but it's what happened.

The Pharisees and Sadducees in the Sanhedrin were right: Christ and his teachings were destructive to their religious, political, and economic status quo. If Christ prevailed, the temple system that gave them power, wealth, and status would disappear. He succeeded. The Romans destroyed the temple in AD 70 and the Jewish homeland ceased to exist for almost nineteen hundred years.

Christianity is no less dangerous and divisive today. It still disrupts the status quo. Its proponents challenge barbaric and monstrous practices. It displaces and does away with the injustice, power, and greed as the normal ways of doing life. Those who have a vested interest in the way things are, no matter how evil, view Christian teachings as dangerous because they are.

Christianity is not violent nor is it a hazardous political or military force. It is incredibly threatening because people who follow Christ are changed at the core of their being. Who they are, what they are, and how they live inevitably seep into culture. His followers subvert the status quo with their new and transformed lives.

To Live an Authentic Life

The unimaginable power of new life was at work in Nicodemus and Joseph of Arimathea. It seems likely they witnessed Christ's arrest, trial, torture, and death. But they may have heard the news like the rest of Jerusalem on Good Friday morning. Those details are lost in the mists of history. But these men left a clear record of what matters most—clear steps that guide all who want to live authentic, courageous lives.

Break with the Past

Nicodemus and Joseph of Arimathea broke with the past by burying Christ. It changed everything. It was a single act at the end of a long process. Both men were at odds with the high priest and the Sanhedrin before Christ's arrest, but the crucifixion brought things to a head. They could not straddle the fence any longer.

> After this Joseph of Arimathea asked Pilate if he could take away the body of Jesus. Joseph was a disciple of Jesus, but a secret one because he feared the Jewish authorities. Pilate gave him permission, so he came and took the body away. (John 19:38)

People try to hold disparate and dissonant parts of life together, but the tension inevitably builds to a breaking point. They must choose to be one thing or the other. No amount of rationalizing restores harmony. Some try to hold on to their faith in Christ and their love for the world. It simply can't be done.

Act Courageously

Joseph of Arimathea "was secretly a disciple of Jesus for fear of the Jews, [but he] took courage and went to Pilate and asked for the body of Jesus" (Luke 19:38). It took bravery for Nicodemus to join the effort. Both men believed in Jesus privately out of fear. After Jesus's death, both acted with courage, knowing they would invite the wrath of the most powerful people and institutions of their day.

Most people don't think of themselves as particularly brave so they play it safe. But without courage we abandon any hope of living authentic lives. Courage isn't the property of the extraordinary few. Courage is the extraordinary path of ordinary people.

Live a Public Faith

There was no way to keep what the two of them did a secret. Pilate and Herod knew. The chief priest and the Sanhedrin knew. The whole city knew. As important members of the Sanhedrin, Joseph and Nicodemus did not agree with or support its decision. Their power and prestige added credibility to Christ's life and teachings. Their actions proved their faith.

Nicodemus and Joseph of Arimathea made Easter possible. Had Christ's body been left to rot and then unceremoniously thrown into the city dump, there would have been no open and empty tomb, no eyewitnesses, and the women would not have come Easter morning to care for his body. The story of Easter would have been dramatically different without their great and public courage.

Going public makes all the difference. Authentic living puts who we are and what we truly believe on display in dramatic and powerful ways. People often notice and honor the courage, caring, and sacrifice of those who live authentic lives even when they disagree with them.

Invest

It cost Joseph and Nicodemus to follow Christ and they paid the price. It's impossible to know what the shroud and pounds of spices cost. But that's not the way to measure their investment. They put all they had—their reputations, positions, status, futures, and money—on the line for their faith in Christ. They stopped playing it safe, gave what it took to get the job done, and demonstrated one of the most basic requirements of an authentic, courageous life.

> Nicodemus . . . brought a mixture of myrrh and aloe, nearly seventy-five pounds in all. Following Jewish burial customs, they took Jesus' body and wrapped it, with the spices, in linen cloths. (John 19:39-40)

For a time, Nicodemus and Joseph of Arimathea believed openly following Jesus cost too much and benefited them too little. If their present was all that mattered, following Jesus was a really bad investment.

Investment is a present cost with the hope of future greater gain. Their future was more important than holding on to what they had. The difference between a good or bad investment is the trustworthiness of the one offering the investment. No one was or ever will be more trustworthy than Jesus (Matthew 6:19-21; Mark 10:29-31).

Expect to Sacrifice

Purchasing a shroud and spices may have been an expensive investment, but for these rich men the amount probably didn't rise to the level of sacrifice. But Joseph of Arimathea sacrificed his own new tomb. Such tombs, carved into stone, were extremely expensive and intended for multigenerational family burials. Bodies were laid in crypts cut into the wall or on low benches until they decomposed. Then their bones were gathered into ossuaries with the name of the deceased carved on the outside to make room for the next burial.

Joseph sacrificed something of great value to benefit another and the greater good.

> There was a garden in the place where Jesus was crucified, and in the garden was a new tomb in which no one had ever been laid. Because

it was the Jewish Preparation Day and the tomb was nearby, they laid
Jesus in it. (John 19:41-42)

All who pursue an authentic life make sacrifices. The gospel always has
and always will advance because brave men and women willingly sacrifice that
which is of greatest value in order to benefit the cause of Christ. They are our
examples and our heroes.

They frighten us. We fear what taking that path could cost. We fear we
lack the courage, the commitment, and the character to live like our heroes.

Afterward

W̶e don't know what happened to Nicodemus and Joseph of Arimathea after Good Friday. They disappear from the Gospels and aren't mentioned elsewhere in the New Testament. Apart from some legends and myths, we know nothing about them. What we do know is that they stopped pretending and lived courageous, authentic lives.

Pretenders, fakes, frauds, and failures are welcome at the open tomb. Easter is the towering story of God's pure and authentic love. That truth beckons to us through the fog of doubt and deceit that shrouds so much of life. His love, forgiveness, and grace are real. The hope and promise of Easter are real. His presence, patience, and compassion are real. All of this, all that Easter proclaims, is the truest truth. In that certainty we find the power to live joy-filled and authentic lives. We may be pretenders, but God isn't. Easter proves it.

Jesus in the Supermarket, 1988

March 27—Palm Sunday
April 1—Good Friday
April 3—Easter Sunday

Riding in the basket near the handle of the shopping cart, the boy faced his mom. His feet dangled and bounced in time with her steps. While she scanned the shelves in front of her, he peered down the aisle behind them. That day she added Easter candy, a chocolate bunny, and an egg-dyeing kit to the cart.

Pushing his cart, a man rounded the corner behind them. He had the bewildered look of a man sent on a shopping expedition by his wife. He didn't have a clue where to find most of what she wanted! So he walked down every aisle, matching his list with items on the shelves. It was his fourth trip down this aisle.

The only part of the store he was personally familiar with was the bakery, where a cup of coffee and a donut were a dollar. It was the best deal in town.

When the man came into view, the little boy let out a cry of joy at the top of his lungs. "Look, Mommy, there's Jesus!"

The boy might as well have said, "There's Elvis!" Every head within earshot turned in the direction of the boy's outstretched arms and mile-wide grin. Shocked by the outburst, his mother turned around just in time to see the look on the man's face change from bewildered to shocked and then to amused.

"No, honey," she said, "that's Mr. Burkhart."

"No, Mommy," he insisted, "that's Jesus!"

The man smiled and approached the mother and boy.

"I'm so sorry, Mr. Burkhart! I don't know what's got into him."

"It's all right. I've been called a lot worse."

"Hi!" Burkhart said to the boy as he reached out and picked him up. The boy fit easily into his arms, gave him a big hug, and then leaned back, put one hand on each side of the man's face, and declared, "I see you, Jesus!"

The adults exchanged pleasantries for a few more minutes while he held her son.

"Well, I've got to go! My wife will think I got lost," he said with a smile as he placed his young friend back into his mother's shopping cart.

"By the way, do you know where they hide the baking soda?"

"Aisle 13, with the other baking supplies," she answered.

"Thanks! Bye-bye!" Burkhart said, waving at the boy.

"Bye-bye, Jesus!" shouted the little man as he waved with all his might, more convinced than ever that his theological convictions were well founded and that he had indeed experienced a supermarket theophany.

Burkhart smiled, gently shook his head, and pushed his cart to the end of the aisle. He turned the wrong way if he was going to aisle 13 but the right way if he was headed for another donut.

It took the young mother a little while to figure out the strange case of mistaken identity. When she finally teased out the truth, she decided her son had come to a perfectly logical (for a three-year-old) conclusion.

On Sundays Mr. Burkhart was the assistant Sunday school superintendent at their church. One of his duties was to visit each classroom, make sure everything was going well and that the teachers had what they needed. There was nothing more important, as far as he was concerned, than seeing the next generation come to love and serve the God who means so much to him.

On his Sunday rounds Burkhart did one other thing: he picked up the offerings.

Each Sunday the young mother or his father put a few coins in the boy's pocket with strict instructions to "give the money to Jesus." Each Sunday her son did exactly that and each Sunday "Jesus" showed up to get his offering!

Then much to her son's delight, "Jesus" showed up in the supermarket!

When she reminded me of this story at my father's funeral, she was thankful my dad wasn't a pretender and she didn't have to worry that her son would see "Jesus" saying or doing something the real Jesus wouldn't do or say.

So am I.

Chapter 6

The Great Exchange

Judica

5th Sunday in Lent—Passion Sunday

Introit
Judica me, Deus
Judge me, O God.
Psalm 43:1 (KJV)

Judge me, O God, and plead my cause against an ungodly nation: O deliver
me from the deceitful and unjust man.
For thou art the God of my strength: why dost thou cast me off? why go I
mourning because of the oppression of the enemy?
Psalm 43:1-2 (KJV)

Freedom is from within.
—Frank Lloyd Wright

Reprieve

It wouldn't be long now.

He had waited months for the day they would kill him. Each morning brought him a little closer to the miserable end of a miserable life. He was glad it would be over but terrified by the way it would end.

He was an insurrectionist, a thief, and a murderer. His cell mates were just common thieves. But Dysmas and Gestas would die with him. Gestas railed against the Romans in stunning, vulgar, multilingual torrents. Terror crouched behind his rage.

Dysmas? Dysmas joined the rioters hoping to loot some shops and scamper home with his stolen booty. He was in the wrong place at the wrong time and got caught. Dysmas sobbed for days after his arrest. Now he sat in the dark, staring at the stone walls. He prayed. He cried. But mostly he gently rocked back and forth.

Sunset. Tomorrow morning they would die. Passover was over and the Sabbath was coming—just enough time to squeeze in a crucifixion or two. Not that the Romans cared. They just didn't want more trouble with the Jews.

Sleep came and he dreamed of freedom.

The rising sun streamed through the narrow slit and filled the dungeon with dim light. He woke and looked around. He was still here. Freedom was only a cruel dream. Dysmas lay curled up like a baby. Gestas paced in the corner farthest from the door.

That's when he heard the commotion in the courtyard. A prisoner was dragged before Pilate. The courtyard was full of angry men milling around, muttering threats and curses. He couldn't hear it all but it seemed to him that they wanted the Romans to crucify someone else. Well, the more the merrier. What was one more dead Jew to the Romans anyway?

The crowd milled around the courtyard waiting for Pilate's entrance. Inside, Pilate paced and pondered his wife's strange warning about the Rabbi he had interrogated and sent away. Pilate had been cleverly and successfully manipulated and he knew it. He couldn't win. The man wasn't guilty of anything except angering the Sanhedrin. But if he released the Rabbi they'd say he was not loyal to Caesar, and Pilate was already in trouble with Tiberius. His men were ready, but he didn't want the bloody repercussions of putting down a riot.

All he could do was try. But he was a prisoner to an angry mob and those who demanded the Rabbi's death. He was trapped.

Pilate stepped out and faced the crowd.

Suddenly the crowd quieted. Pilate spoke. "I find no guilt in him."

"Crucify him!" someone shouted and the crowd roared its mindless approval.

Pilate waited, and then he shouted over the low rumblings of the angry crowd, "You have a custom that I should release one man for you at the Passover. Do you want me to release Jesus Barabbas or Jesus who is called Christ?"

"Not this man, but Barabbas!" someone screamed back.

"Barabbas! Barabbas!" The crowd picked up the chant. "Barabbas!" "Barabbas!"

"Then what shall I do with Jesus who is called Christ, the king of the Jews?"

"Let him be crucified!" someone shouted.

"Why, what evil has he done?"

"Crucify him, crucify him!" The words echoed in waves across the courtyard.

"I found no guilt deserving death in him. I will punish and release him."

"No! Let him be crucified!"

"I am innocent of this man's blood; see to it yourselves!"

"His blood is on us and on our children!" they screamed.

Had the crowd really chosen him over the Rabbi from Nazareth? Had the great Roman governor been cowed by a bunch of unarmed Jews and given in to them? It couldn't be true.

From somewhere deep inside a nervous giggle erupted into hysterical laughter.

Footsteps echoed in the hall. Swords clinked against armor. Keys rattled. The lock turned. The door creaked open.

Roman guards came in, their drawn swords a phalanx of steel protecting the centurion who followed them. The officer looked at the three with unmistakable and murderous disgust.

"Which of you is Barabbas?"

"I am," he said.

"Let's go."

So it was time. One way or the other it would soon be over.

He walked out of the cell, down the narrow dark hallway surrounded by the Romans, and into the courtyard. Three crosses leaned against the wall. The post where prisoners were tied when they were scourged stood in the center of a semicircle of blood-spattered sand dotted with bits of rotting flesh. A soldier lazily took a few practice swings. He was very skilled and no doubt loved his work, but practice made perfect.

Barabbas walked past the crosses, past the whipping post, to the courtyard gate. The great door swung open in front of him. It wasn't a dream. It was true. Pilate kept his word. He was going free.

"Get out!" the centurion barked as he threw a filthy cloak at his feet.

When Barabbas stooped to pick the cloak out of the dirt, the Roman stepped close and crouched next to him.

"I'll see you again," the centurion snarled. "You may have gotten away with it this time but you'll be back. I know your kind. I'll be waiting. Believe me . . . I'll be waiting."

As he stood, Barabbas noticed the beaten and bleeding prisoner near the crosses. He had collapsed in the dirt and was surrounded by his Roman tormentors. They had viciously scourged him. The purple cloak draped around his shoulders was caked with drying blood. His face was swollen from the beatings, and large dark scabs had formed where they had ripped out clumps of his beard and hair. A crudely fashioned crown of thorns had been driven into his scalp and rivulets of blood ran down his cheeks.

Their eyes met. The man smiled.

He smiled? How could he smile? He must know . . . it should be me, Barabbas thought.

The centurion roughly shoved him and Barabbas stumbled through the gate as Gestas was dragged, screaming and cursing, to the whipping post. Dysmas was not far behind, praying, whimpering, begging, and calling out to God for forgiveness. Barabbas didn't dare and couldn't stand to look back. The scourge whistled through the air, the metal- and bone-tipped lashes bit into soft flesh with a sickening thud and Gestas cried out in agony.

He stepped through the gate and into the street. The great doors closed behind him. It was done. The exchange was complete. He would live. The Rabbi would die.

Barabbas covered his head with the cloak, ducked into the anonymity of the crowd, and disappeared.

Jesus Barabbas

Matthew 27:15-26; Mark 15:6-15; Luke 23:13-24; John 18:38b-40

People protect freedom when they have it and demand freedom when they don't. They fiercely insist on the right to decide and to do what they want, resist confinement and physical restraint, and reject external control, regulation, or interference in their lives.

Freedom does not guarantee its wise use. Some use freedom to create, contribute—to build lives and legacies, to bless and benefit. Others use freedom to destroy and demean, to take and terrorize, to steal and hoard. The misuse of freedom inevitably, predictably, and ultimately leads to the loss of freedom. Barabbas used his freedom without regard to the consequences and so lost it.

Unraveling Freedom

Our deep need to be free raises great questions about the nature of freedom itself.

Freedom is a capacity, not a moral category. It is a gift from our wise and loving God intended for our joy. But much of the misery people inflict on each other could be avoided if we weren't free to live outside God's boundaries. Surely the God who created heaven and earth, who created all reality, could have managed that. It would have been easier for him too. So why grant us freedom in the first place?

Perhaps the best and truest answer is that God knows and we don't. It's not a very satisfying answer. There may be other reasons.

Freedom reflects God's nature. We are free because our Creator is infinitely and absolutely free. He can literally do anything, at any time and in any way he wishes. He has written that joyous quality into the deepest core of all he created. Freedom makes the exuberant chaos of creativity possible. We do not blindly execute the great programmer's code. We interact with the environment, learn, and re-create our world because we are free.

Freedom is essential. We live on a dynamic planet that constantly remakes itself through dramatic and powerful natural forces. Great political, economic, and societal forces change culture, societies, and our day-to-day lives. If we were not free we could not survive long in such a wild and wonderful world.

Freedom is not sinful. We are not free because we are sinners. We are sinners because we use the glorious capacity and gift of freedom to sin. Adam and Eve were sinless and free when they tried to shake off God's limits and steal deity and immortality. Freedom was the means, not the problem.

The Prisoner Barabbas

Here's everything we know about Barabbas.

Barabbas was on death row, probably in a dungeon inside the Fortress Antonia, when he suddenly appears in the Easter story. We don't know how long he'd been in prison, but he wasn't going to be there much longer. He'd lost his freedom and was about to lose his life when the angry mob pressured Pilate into an unthinkable prisoner exchange. Guilty Jesus Barabbas went free. Innocent Jesus of Nazareth took his cross and his place on Golgotha.

> It was customary during the festival for the governor to release to the crowd one prisoner, whomever they might choose. At that time there was a well-known prisoner named Jesus Barabbas. (Matthew 27:15-16)

Barabbas was not just imprisoned by the thick, cold, stone walls of his dungeon and burly Roman soldiers. His true prison was one of his own making.

Three forces drove Barabbas in a destructive direction: his past, his uncontrolled life, and his own choices.

1. His Past

Barabbas was a prisoner to his past.

Barabbas literally means the "son of the father" (*bar*—son of, and *abba*—father). It was common to identify a particular person by naming his father. Jesus used a similar construction to identify Peter as Simon Bar-Jonah (Matthew 16:17). A Jewish false prophet living in Paphos on Cyprus was identified as Bar-Jesus (Acts 13:6). Even today Jewish boys participate in the rite of *bar Mitzvah* to become "a son of the Commandment."

Sometimes *bar-abbas* was used to say a boy was like his father. Perhaps Jesus Barabbas really was like his father and crime was the family business. But it could be a more cutting insult. If a boy's father was unknown the boy would be referred to *bar-abbas*, an illegitimate child. Either way it wasn't a compliment.

We can imagine an angry young man growing up in a culture where the circumstances of his birth were shrouded in shame, and he experienced the taunts of other boys, the demeaning looks of the village women, the giggles of the girls, and the crude jokes the village men told about his mother. Maybe he preferred life as an insurrectionist, a thief, and a murderer rather than as an illegitimate son or the spawn of a criminal. We can't know for sure.

Prisons forged in the past are out of our control. Some grow up protected and adored. Others are preyed upon and abused. Some grow healthy and strong. Some are born damaged by illness or accident. Much of life contains events and circumstances we cannot and would not choose. But the realities of the past confine our present and restrain the future whether or not we like it or want it.

2. His Uncontrolled Life

Barabbas was imprisoned by an out-of-control life and disregard for others. Some want to turn Barabbas into a proto–Robin Hood, a patriot, and a romantic and heroic figure. More likely he was a thief and murderer and opportunistic looter.

We all forge prison bars from the strong steel of our emotions. Hatred, bitterness, envy, and resentment inflame our hearts, imprison our minds, and cage our lives. When those feelings grow out of control we lose the light of reason in the thicket of pain. We are driven to vengeance, rage, and perhaps violence.

Sometimes we lash out at those who have hurt us, those who look as if they might hurt us, or anyone who is near. Sometimes we turn our hostility inward. Self-loathing and self-condemnation are strong prisons that keep us from becoming the persons we dream of and are created to be. We cement those prison bars into the foundations of our lives by our own hands.

3. His Choices and Conduct

Barabbas forged his prison bars with his choices and conduct. Barabbas stole from someone, killed someone, rioted, and joined an insurrection.

We create facts with our choices and conduct. Those facts can become prisons that define our present and limit the future. We blame the past, our pain, and those who caused it. We hold everyone and everything, including God, accountable. We argue that it's not really our fault. We just played the hand dealt us from a stacked deck.

It sounds good. It makes people feel better. Too bad it isn't true.

People can and do forge their own prison bars. The unwed mother did not choose the confines and responsibilities of parenthood but chose sex with her boyfriend. The alcoholic did not choose the prison of addiction but chose to drink. The crippled young man did not choose life in a wheelchair but chose to drive fast and drunk.

At some moment reality breaks through. We cannot be who we want to be and the lives we long for are tantalizingly out of reach. We chafe in our chains, reach through the bars, cry out against the injustices of life, and hunger to be free. But we forged those bars and chains.

We reap what we sow. Sometimes we choose what liberates and enables us. Sometimes we choose what enslaves us, disables us, damages others, and destroys the future. Sometimes we act with honor and gain the respect and trust that frees us.

Barabbas killed someone. There is another kind of killing that does not leave a lifeless victim. The body lives but the soul dies. All we need are words or a lie. Cruel or unthinking parents strangle the souls and destroy the futures of their children. Their victims die slowly from the inside out in the grip of the endless and daily barrage of verbal venom, physical abuse, or sexual assault.

Barabbas was a thief. All of us have taken what was not ours and have had someone take what we did not give. Some have lost possessions. Things can be replaced; they are just things. Many have had what is much more precious stolen—their reputations, dignity, self-esteem, and love. One is no less a thief because they did not steal something tangible.

Barabbas was a rebel. We are a race of rebels and have been so since Eve picked the fruit in the garden of Eden in defiance of God's will and word. We are rebels with only one cause—our pride. We often stand against social convention and rightful authority not to undo some great evil, but because we want what we want; we want it now, and God help you if you get in our way. There is nothing noble or redeeming in such rebellion.

There is no crueler tyranny, no prison more confining, and no situation more hopeless than always having to have your own way. Such selfishness brings us into confrontation with every authority and defines and destroys every relationship. We may get what we want, but we lose what matters most.

No. Barabbas was not free. He was not free even after he was freed.

The Prisoner Pilate

Matthew 27:1-2, 11-26; Mark 15:1-20; Luke 23:1-25; John
18:28–19:18

On that day, the fates of two men rested in the hands of a third. The Roman prefect, Pontius Pilate, governor of Judea with three thousand Roman soldiers under his command, sat at the pinnacle of power. He is the most enigmatic and confusing character in the story. With the wealth and might of the world's most powerful empire at his disposal, with the great status of his office Pilate should have been free.

> When the crowd had come together, Pilate asked them, "Whom would you like me to release to you, Jesus Barabbas or Jesus who is called Christ?" He knew that the leaders of the people had handed him over because of jealousy. While he was serving as judge, his wife sent this message to him, "Leave that righteous man alone. I've suffered much today in a dream because of him." (Matthew 27:17-19)

But Pilate was not free. Invisible bonds held him as tightly as the enraged mob held Jesus or the dungeon held Barabbas. This was the signature moment of his life. Nothing he did before or after would matter as much as this one decision. He is not remembered for all he accomplished as a Roman governor but for trying to wash away his responsibility for the murder of history's only truly innocent man.

> But the chief priests and the elders persuaded the crowds to ask for Barabbas and kill Jesus. The governor said, "Which of the two do you want me to release to you?"

"Barabbas," they replied.

Pilate said, "Then what should I do with Jesus who is called Christ?"

They all said, "Crucify him!"

But he said, "Why? What wrong has he done?"

They shouted even louder, "Crucify him!" (Matthew 27:20-23)

Like Barabbas, Pilate found himself in a prison of his own making. Four issues kept him under lock and key.

1. His Fear

Pilate was a prisoner to fear. During his tenure as governor of Judea, Pilate was reprimanded by the emperor and had reason to fear the wrath of Tiberius. When the chief priests accused Jesus of sedition—that he advocated not giving tribute to Caesar—the trap was set. When Pilate wavered and seemed on the verge of letting Jesus go they reminded him, "If you release this man, you are not Caesar's friend" (John 19:12).

It wasn't an empty threat. The mere hint that Pilate was not loyal to Caesar meant the end of his career and perhaps his life. Faced with that choice, Pilate let fear triumph.

The walls of fear are high and thick. Sometimes what we fear isn't real or isn't likely to happen. Sometimes what we fear is very real. But fear doesn't have to be sensible to paralyze and hold us in its iron grip. It needs only to exist.

2. His Selfishness

Pilate was a prisoner to selfishness. There was nothing in it for him if he freed Jesus. If he did the right thing, it would cost him. He could lose control of the crowd, have a riot on his hands, and lose the support of the Jewish leaders and Herod. It would not advance his career or his life. Justice was not in his best interest. Another crucified Jewish rabbi and rabble-rouser? Not a problem. Where's that basin of water?

Pilate saw that he was getting nowhere and that a riot was starting. So he took water and washed his hands in front of the crowd. "I'm innocent of this man's blood," he said. "It's your problem." (Matthew 27:24)

Acting selfishly feels like acting freely. We do what we want and get what we want—at least it feels that way. Those who only want to know "What's in it for me?" inhabit a particularly miserable prison and endure a thousand painful cuts to heart and soul. Selfishness blinds us to our true self-interest, the worth and value of others, and guarantees misery.

3. His Need to Please People

Pilate was a prisoner to his need to please the Jewish leaders, mend fences with Herod, and cement his relationship with Tiberius. He was glad to please the crowd and his soldiers. Pilate's pathological people-pleasing reveals the lie that forged the bars of his private prison. He believed happiness, success, and worth depended on others. Making sure that others were pleased and also that they valued him ensured his future.

Everyone wants to be liked, to be well thought of, and to please people he or she cares for or loves. These normal and healthy impulses aren't the issue. There is nothing wrong with wanting to make someone happy or doing something good for somebody else. In the end they are pleased and so are we. But that's not Pilate.

4. His Denial of Responsibility

Pilate was a prisoner to his fear of responsibility. Pilate had the power to set Jesus free—to act on what he knew was true. Jesus was an innocent man, falsely accused, and the victim of a jealous plot, and Pilate knew it. Pilate could free anyone he wished. He just wasn't man enough. When he found out Jesus was from Nazareth, he sent him to Herod to shift the responsibility. When he argued that Jesus should be freed he pointed out that Herod agreed with him

(Luke 23:14-16). When he caved in to the crowd's preposterous demands he called for a basin of water, washed his hands, and said he wasn't to blame. It wasn't true.

> All the people replied, "Let his blood be on us and on our children."
> Then he released Barabbas to them. He had Jesus whipped, then handed him over to be crucified. (Matthew 27:25-26)

When we refuse to take responsibility and blame others, we enter a prison with armed guards. It begins with the lie of powerlessness and grows into believing we have no choice. No one can make anyone do anything. They can only make them wish they had. Ceding control, refusing to take responsibility, and blaming others enslaves. It doesn't free.

Finding freedom means coming to grips with the hard reality that we are responsible for our attitudes, affections, and actions. When we deny that truth we are imprisoned by our fear, by our desire to please others, by our selfishness, or by our own willing blindness to our responsibility.

Jesus Who Is Free

At the end of that day one man walked out of prison, one man held court in his palace, and one man was stripped of his freedom and dignity and murdered. But only one was free. Jesus is the one truly free man in the Easter story. Unlike Barabbas he was not ruled by his past, anger, greed, hopelessness, hatred, or rebellion. Unlike Pilate he was not controlled by fear, selfishness, the slavish need to please others, or refusal to take responsibility.

Freedom of this sort is rare but not impossible. "So if the Son makes you free, you will be free indeed" (John 8:36). Perhaps we can be free too.

The Bible gives us a general principle about freedom: we are slaves to what we practice, what we submit to, and what we allow to overcome us (John 8:34; 2 Peter 2:19; Romans 6:16; Galatians 5:1). Slavery of this kind is both a choice and a condition. We may choose it a little at a time, but we still choose it.

Temptation begins in the heart and mind. But when we act on that temptation we trade freedom for slavery. We follow the call of what we know is wrong until we grow deaf to what is right. The din of the world drowns out the voice of God. Sin entangles and overwhelms us. We are compelled to follow its wishes and our cravings.

It is the pattern of all addiction. The call is sweet and satisfying. The first steps are exciting and filled with pleasure. The more we get, the more we want until it is all we want. Soon our lives are totally and inextricably enmeshed with our desire. We are its slaves.

The Book of Common Prayer contains this petition: "From all inordinate and sinful affections; and from all the deceits of the world, the flesh and the devil, Good Lord, deliver us." (*The Litany or General Supplication: To be used after the Third Collect at Morning or Evening Prayer*)

The petition is for deliverance from "inordinate and sinful affections" and "deceits." Our natural desires aren't the problem. Slavery is not enjoying and appreciating good gifts from a good God. The slave loves the gifts more than the God who gave them. We believe a lie when we believe these things bring meaning, purpose, and freedom. They don't. They can't. They were never meant to.

Jesus faced the "world, the flesh and the devil" in his wilderness temptation (Matthew 4:1-11) and refused the slavery that came with those temptations. He was free because he was secure in his person, his place, his purpose, his present, and his prospects.

Secure in His Person

Jesus knew who he was and did not need the approval or affirmation of others to bolster his sense of self. He had nothing to prove, no need to self-aggrandize, no desire to be someone else or lead another life. He was not immune to the temptations that prey on our need for the approval of others or to prove our worth and value. But he faced and overcame them.

We are not like him. We have looked deeply into the distorted mirror others hold up and see ourselves that way. We have measured our experiences and failures and determined that we are substandard intellectually, morally, physically, and spiritually. We fear that our carefully constructed facade will crumble and reveal our true and imperfect selves.

Secure in His Place

Jesus knew he was loved and valued by his parents, his followers, and most important, his heavenly Father. He was not striving to find a place to belong or people to love him and was immune to temptations that prey on our need for love, affection, and belonging. He had no need to compromise his freedom to gain a place in the hearts of others.

But many do not feel this secure and are thereby controlled by the fear of rejection and exclusion. Terrified by the thought of being alone, they hide who they are, become what others expect, and are enslaved to their need for love and belonging.

Secure in His Purpose

Jesus knew why he came and the purpose of his life. Many only survive, meet their physical needs, and live as comfortably as possible. Others live with purpose. But all too often that purpose is to achieve, attain, or acquire something, some position, or someone. Making ourselves richer, more prominent, or more powerful ultimately fails to fulfill our deepest needs. We become slaves to what comforts us, to the pursuit of power, status, and wealth, and lose our freedom trying to fill the spaces in our soul.

Secure in His Present

Jesus the wandering rabbi with no place to lay his head was at peace with his circumstances. He knew God cared for the sparrows and would care for him. He was immune to the temptations to gain wealth and power to keep him and those he loved safe. His well-being was in the hands of his great, good, and all-wise Father.

We live in an unsteady and unpredictable world and know we are not truly safe. Forces beyond our control can strip every precious thing from our lives. That reality enslaves us to whatever or whoever we think can keep us safe. But it is a sham. We are truly safe only in God.

Secure in His Prospects

Jesus was at peace with his future. He knew the torturous road to Golgotha lay in front of him. But it was not the end. Another brighter future awaited him—a future that could not be taken from him and would never end. He was immune to the temptations that come to those who see this life as their only life.

The future is unsure and unpredictable. We are taught to value the moment: yesterday is gone, tomorrow has not come, and now is all we have. Whether we want it or not, whether we like it or not, the future is rushing toward us. We are painfully aware of our mortality and the fragility of life, so we become slaves to uncertainty.

Finding Freedom

L ike Jesus we are free only when we discover ourselves in God. The reflection we see in the mirrors others hold, in our experiences, in what others say, and in what we tell ourselves isn't our true self. We know who we are only when we see ourselves through God's eyes.

We are truly free only when we are in right relationship with our Creator. Our struggle to belong ends when we know, ultimately and finally, that we do not belong to any other person, to a race or nation, or even to ourselves. We belong to God and always will. Nothing and no one can separate us from him and his love—except us.

We are truly free only when we give ourselves to our created purpose. People do not exist to be born, make little people, grow old, and die. We were made to participate with the almighty Creator of the universe in his great and glorious cause of redemption and reconciliation. Those who join his great purpose live free, live according to its dictates, and live without regard for the consequences.

We are truly free only when we know we are safe, not because our physical safety will never be threatened but because our lives are guided by the hand of an all-wise, all-powerful, and all-loving Father. The worst we can imagine— cruel martyrdom, a torturous disease, the loss of everything and everyone we hold dear—are circumstances under the control of the one who loves us most. They may happen. But we are safe—in him.

The future is notoriously uncertain and insecure. We cannot know or control it. But we can rest knowing that God holds the remainder of our days here and in the innumerable eons of immortality that follow. So we are free. No one and nothing can take from us what God has promised to us. They can kill us. But they can't take our lives or our freedom.

We belong to God.

The liberating joy of Easter belongs to all of us trapped by the past and our own destructive choices. Jesus came to release prisoners, including each of us, from their chains (Luke 4:18). At Easter we celebrate Christ's victory in the great battle that won our freedom and fulfilled his mission. The chains of our past, our pain, and our sin fall away when we embrace the redeeming love Christ demonstrated that first Easter. In their place we are given the riches of his grace and the joy of his presence. When we believe the truth of the Easter message and trust Christ's work, we discover true and everlasting freedom.

The Ten-Year Bit, 2009

April 5—Palm Sunday
April 10—Good Friday
April 12—Easter Sunday

When I met Curt, he was in the last six months of a ten-year federal prison sentence for manufacturing and distributing methamphetamines across state lines.

I started work as a contractor in a religious program at the Federal Correctional Institution on April 1 that year. I helped prisoners arrange mentoring relationships with others of their faith who would help them make successful transitions back into the community.

I felt like a fool on a fool's errand on April Fool's Day.

At the last minute I was asked to preach in the Protestant chapel on Easter Sunday afternoon. The scheduled speaker was called out of town for a personal emergency and the Protestant chaplain had another commitment.

Following the service I made it a point to shake hands with as many inmates as possible.

"Hey, Doc. I didn't know you were a preacher," said Curt.

I had seen Curt around the unit but hadn't really talked to him. He was about to graduate from the program and there wasn't time to connect him with a mentor.

We chatted for a few minutes. When I learned the twenty-eight-year-old had spent almost a decade in federal lock-up my response was typical: "I'm so sorry."

"I'm not," Curt responded with a smile.

"You're not sorry you're in prison?" I asked, not sure I heard him correctly.

"I'm sorry for what I did but I'm not sorry about coming to prison. It was the best thing that could have happened to me. I'd be dead now if I hadn't been arrested. The guys I ran drugs with in Houston are all dead or in prison or worse."

I wanted to interrupt and ask what was worse than dead or in prison. I didn't.

"Catching this case saved my life. I'm clean and sober. I'm healthy. I'm young. I got my high school diploma and I earned a college degree on the inside. God helped me turn my life around. The way I figure it, I traded ten years of my life for the rest of my life. Sorry? No way!" he said in a way that left no doubt every word was absolutely true.

A corrections officer called the move on the prison loudspeaker and interrupted us. The prisoners had ten minutes to get to their units or where they were supposed to be.

"See you, Doc," Curt said with a smile.

I watched him go, amazed by the smiling, handsome young man in prison khaki, a Bible tucked under his arm, making his way back to his cell behind the razor wire of the Federal Correctional Institution.

"Best thing that ever happened. . . ."

Really.

Chapter 7

The Bystander

Dominica Palmarum

6th Sunday in Lent—Palm Sunday

Introit
Iustus ut palma florebit.
The righteous shall flourish like the palm tree.
Psalm 92:12 (KJV)

The righteous shall flourish like the palm tree:
he shall grow like a cedar in Lebanon.
Those that be planted in the house of the Lord
shall flourish in the courts of our God.
Psalm 92:12-13 (KJV)

The opposite of love is not hate. It's indifference.
—Elie Wiesel

The Bystander

The half-buried nail beckoned.

He bent down and picked it out of the loose dirt. It was slightly bent and looked as if it had lain on the hilltop for a long time—just a rusty old nail. But he knew better. It had been there only a few days and its reddish hue wasn't rust. It was blood—dried, dirt-encrusted blood. As he turned it over and over in his fingers, the events of that day filled his mind and suspended time.

Simon had retraced his steps through the city streets and up the winding path to this monstrous place. Bizarre rumors about the man who died here reverberated throughout the city. His body was missing. Some said his followers stole it to create the illusion that his prophecy of resurrection had come true. It started with a few women who went to care for his body, and then he heard tales about an open tomb, angels, a ghostly apparition, a gardener who wasn't a gardener, and soldiers who said they fell asleep, as if anyone believed that. None of it made any sense.

So he came back to the hilltop. As he took in the scene, surreal images of that day filled his mind. That day began like so many others but ended as the most traumatic and transforming day he had ever seen.

That day, Simon had elbowed his way through to the edge of the road. The macabre parade, just a few yards from him, parted the sea of onlookers as it pressed forward.

Flanked by their executioners, three bloody and beaten prisoners struggled under the weight of their crosses. Suddenly everything stopped. One of the prisoners collapsed directly in front of him. Dried blood crusted his swollen face from deep gashes cut into his scalp by a crudely crafted crown of thorns. A blood-soaked robe draped over his shoulders. A loud thud echoed when the cross hit the stone pavement. The man groaned in agony, as if something deep inside was crushed under the weight of the falling cross and the horror of his torture.

He struggled to lift the cross and rise from the dirt as the Roman nearest him screamed and cursed, kicked and punched, as if a little more brutality would get the prisoner on his feet. It didn't. The prisoner responded by looking fearlessly and deeply into the soldier's eyes and his contorted visage.

The soldier looked up and looked around. Without warning or hesitation the Roman was on him. "Jew, pick up that cross!" he commanded.

Simon would have slipped away if he'd had the chance. But disobeying the Roman wasn't a good idea. Confused and shocked, he hesitated just long enough for the impatient Roman to slap his head, grab his arm, and roughly shove him into the street. Simon offered no resistance and did what he was told. He knelt next to the man and reached for the cross.

"I don't know what you did, but you don't deserve this," Simon whispered.

"Thank you" was the only response the dying man could manage. The words were slurred and there was an ominous rasp in his voice.

As long as he lived, the merchant from Cyrene never forgot those words, the calm tone, or the resolute, determined gaze. He had never seen such naked courage.

The merchant tried to lift the incredibly heavy cross. He was healthy and uninjured but it was almost impossible to lift it from the fallen man's shoulders and onto his own.

"Help him!" ordered the centurion.

Soldiers nearest the merchant sheathed their swords, grabbed the cross, lifted it, and positioned it on the merchant's shoulders.

Simon had no idea where they were going or how far he would have to carry a dying man's cross. But he knew better than to ask for help or complain.

It was a long, difficult walk through the streets and up the winding path to the top of the hill. He had heard of this area—the place of the skull, Golgotha.

The merchant dropped the cross where he was told, stepped back, and took in the scene.

He took a couple more steps back to blend into the crowd.

He watched in horror as the soldiers stripped the prisoners of their clothing and dignity and forced them to lie naked on the crosses. The three-man execution teams worked quickly and efficiently. They'd clearly done this before, many times. It didn't take long. Neat. Efficient. Roman! Then they gathered up their tools and sat in a small circle near the edge of the killing ground and gambled.

When the horrors threatened to stretch past sundown—a violation of the Sabbath—a soldier picked up a mallet and expertly smashed the legs of two prisoners just below the knee. It kept them from lifting their bodies to grab one more desperate, ragged breath. The third man was already dead. One of them ran a spear into his side just to be sure. Blood and gore splashed on the Roman's hands and feet.

The crowds drifted away. Not much left to see. Simon stayed. Late in the afternoon two Pharisees and their servants claimed his body. One of the few remaining spectators told him they were leaders of the Sanhedrin, Nicodemus and Joseph, who were from a nearby town of Arimathea. They shouldn't have come at all but they did.

They worked quickly to take him from his cross. Dried blood and dirt were lovingly sponged away until all but the most visible signs of his ordeal faded.

"Hurry."

They carefully laid his body on the lower half of the shroud, crossed his hands on his lower abdomen, positioned the chinstrap and face cloth, and applied the spices. Then they draped the upper half of the shroud over the top of his body. Working from his head to his feet, they expertly tucked and folded it until it fit snugly around his form. They tied strips of linen around his ankles, knees, waist, and chest and set out for the tomb.

Simon followed the men to the tomb where the Romans waited. The Jews maneuvered the body through the small, low opening. When they came out the servants pushed a large, rounded stone across the entrance into the ramp-like trench in front of the opening with a dull thud. Gravity made it easy to roll the stone into the trench and almost impossible to push it out.

Then the centurion reached into a small bag slung over his shoulder and pulled out a ball of wax and sealed the tomb. Anyone breaking the seal was subject to Roman "justice."

The centurion ordered his men out of the garden. The merchant slipped away too.

The Jewish temple guards began their vigil.

Simon stayed in Jerusalem. It was the Sabbath and he had business in the city.

Now Simon stood again on the hill, fingering a bent nail and thinking about the strange rumors and the man whose cross he'd carried. Maybe he should stay longer. There was a lot he didn't know and a lot more he wanted to know. He'd never been in Jerusalem for Pentecost. Maybe he'd stay until then.

Simon from Cyrene

Matthew 27:30-32; Mark 15:19-21; Luke 23:24-26

Simon the Cyrene was in Jerusalem the day Christ died. Based on his name and the fact that he was in Jerusalem for the Passover, we assume he was Jewish. Because Cyrene was in North Africa (modern Libya), some think Simon was a black African convert to Judaism. But it's more likely that Simon was a Jewish ex-patriot living in a city on the Mediterranean coast founded by the Greeks and ruled by the Romans.

For a few hours, the orbit of his life brought him into redemption's gravitational field and he carried Christ's cross to Golgotha. Simon was a spectator who participated in the greatest adventure of all time—God's unfolding work of redemption.

> Simon, a man from Cyrene, Alexander and Rufus's father, was coming in from the countryside. They forced him to carry his cross. (Mark 15:21)

Nothing indicates Simon was a follower of Jesus or that he had any interest in the crucifixion of two thieves and a rabbi. Cyrene was a long way from Jerusalem and travel was difficult, dangerous, and expensive. Perhaps he was going to the temple to sacrifice, making his Passover pilgrimage, keeping a business appointment, sightseeing, or meeting friends. If a frustrated Roman soldier had not singled him out, he would have watched the ghoulish spectacle pass, gone on about his business, and faded into history's dusty pages as just another unknown face in the crowd.

Most of the time we are spectators watching the great events of life. Wars are won or lost—most stare from the sidelines. Political candidates rise and fall—many people don't vote. Great companies wax and wane. Monumental cultural shifts shake the foundations of society—most people just try to keep their footing and go on about their business.

Like Simon, most of us lead our lives from the sidelines. Why? It contradicts some of our deepest desires. Perhaps there are some clues in Simon's story.

Focus

Simon's focus was elsewhere. The Bible tells us that Simon came into Jerusalem from the countryside but not why he came. He was focused on his agenda and not on the crucifixion of the Rabbi from Nazareth. He had his own plans, possibilities, and problems.

We focus on our lists. Our work, our family, our hobbies, our dreams, and myriad other concerns fill our minds and blur our vision. Concentration on those things means we ignore much of what is going on around us.

Expectations

Whatever Simon expected walking through the city gates that morning, it certainly wasn't what confronted him. The gruesome spectacle in the streets shocked him.

Life is full of surprises. But often people see what they expect to see and are blind to everything else. Life is an optical illusion and our expectations shape reality. Opportunities for greatness float by, but people don't expect them and they don't see them. We see what we missed only in retrospect and sometimes not even then.

Disguised Opportunities

The opportunity to play a part in the redemption story came disguised as an interruption, a bloody robe, a crown of thorns, and a rough-hewn cross.

It didn't look like treasure. Nothing in that street made Simon want to take up the cross. He may have been a kind and compassionate man, but nothing suggests he looked for that assignment.

Taking up that cross brought Simon very close to the Roman sword. It cost him time and maybe much more. He carried Christ's cross without remuneration or respect. There was nothing in it for him. The experience was risky.

Great opportunities can come disguised in pain, disappointment, loss, and despair. But that doesn't mean they aren't powerful possibilities. It only means people have trouble seeing through the disguise. An engaged life seems dangerous and costly. We are asked, without guarantees, to risk what we cannot lose and pay a price we cannot afford. It may seem futile and fruitless. But no great thing is ever accomplished without great risk.

Direction

The experience took him in a very different direction. Simon was headed into Jerusalem. The execution squad was headed out. Simon was forced to change direction—to go a new way. There was no certainty about how long it would take or what would happen when he got there.

Every life has direction and momentum. We are going somewhere and make plans along the way. Changing course doesn't make sense. Persistence can make us successful. A change in direction threatens that success with no guarantee of our ending up in a better place.

The Bible is full of stories of the men and women who didn't stay on the sidelines. They lived fulfilling and engaged lives. It is also full of those who stood by and missed their opportunities. They could have lived great lives and done tremendous things but didn't. The only real question is on which side of that line will we live?

We have a choice: we can remain spectators watching the rest of the world go by, or we can step into the world, take up our cross, and make a difference.

What does it take to live a fully engaged life?

An Engaged Life

In Simon's story we find six distinct stages that transformed Simon from a bystander to an active participant. In them we find clues to escaping a life lived on the sidelines.

Stage 1: Discovery

The Roman soldier who led Christ found Simon. The root word translated "found" means "to find, learn, or discover" especially after searching.

It's easy to imagine that moment. Christ collapsed and the soldier faced a dilemma. He had to get the prisoners to Golgotha with their crosses and this one couldn't make the trek. He scanned the crowd and spotted Simon. Maybe Simon was close, looked fit enough to carry the cross, or was just in the wrong place at the right time.

The soldier found Simon. But Simon discovered Christ. It must have been a shock to step from the crowd and come close enough to Christ to pick up the cross, hear his groans, and smell the sweat and blood. Simon found a tortured and dying man face down in the dirt under the heavy heel of Roman justice. But Simon didn't really discover Jesus that day. He found a single piece of an epic mosaic. As far as we know, this was the only Jesus Simon ever knew.

Finding and being found are critical to the story of our lives. Believers have been found, not by a burly Roman soldier with a bad attitude, but by the grace and love of Christ. We were wandering, on our way somewhere else, when we crossed paths with Christ. When most people find Jesus they find the Jesus they are looking for—the one they want to find—the Jesus they need or think they need. But when we meet Jesus, we never find all there is to discover. Encountering the Jesus of the Bible makes everything change. It can take a lifetime. It can happen in an instant.

When we discover our Creator and his noble purposes, we can fully engage in life. We must discover our call in order to commit to it.

Stage 2: Captivated

Luke wrote that the Roman seized Simon. The word translated "seized" means "to lay hold of, or to take hold of sometimes with hostile intent." The Roman soldier didn't just order Simon to pick up the cross. He grabbed him and roughly shoved him toward Christ and the cross. Simon's attention and focus were captured. He was riveted to that spot and that moment.

In a world filled with bright and shiny distractions something—anything—that seizes and holds our attention for long is rare. The constant flood of tragedy and titillation of the twenty-four-hour news cycle numbs the heart and mind. We long for a compelling vision that grips the heart and soul and demands our very best. Many never find it. Many stop looking for it. But those who find it, those whose lives are seized by a great passion, a great love, or a great adventure, live in the extraordinary realm of those who are truly alive.

Sadly the message of Easter has been pasteurized and packaged, massaged and marketed until it is no longer the wild, beautiful, and majestic truth that seizes the heart and captures the imagination. The visceral, gritty truth of God becoming man, being tortured, and bleeding on his way to redeem the world, has become another bland ancient fable. We are not gripped by the truth because we have not discovered the truth. But when we do, when we really see Jesus, we are held spellbound by his glory and wonder.

What holds our attention draws us into lives lived to the fullest. Until we are captivated by a great cause, we cannot know the joy of great commitment.

Stage 3: Compelled

Simon was compelled to carry the cross. The armed and threatening Roman soldier didn't make a request, a suggestion, or a polite inquiry. He forced Simon to pick up the cross.

Those who discover and are gripped by the wonder of Christ's story are compelled to act, not out of a threat or fear, but out of a deep longing to be part of the adventure. They cannot resist the joy and grandeur of a life lived with such passion. They don't fear what God will do to them if they don't act. They fear being left out or left behind.

That compulsion is the driving force behind a truly engaging life. The thrill of discovering all we can do and be in God drives us on when we are captivated by the wonder of a life lived to the fullest in God and energized by the Holy Spirit.

Step 4: Action

The Gospel writers agree Simon carried Christ's cross, but they don't say it the same way. Matthew and Mark say that Simon took up the cross. The word they used means "to raise, or lift up—to take away or remove—to take upon oneself and carry what has been raised."

When read that way it conjures up the familiar passion play image. Christ fell under the weight of the cross. Dragged into the street, Simon reached down, lifted the cross from Christ's bloody back, raised it to his own shoulders, and carried it to Golgotha.

> As they led Jesus away, they grabbed Simon, a man from Cyrene, who was coming in from the countryside. They put the cross on his back and made him carry it behind Jesus. (Luke 23:26)

Luke implies someone, probably soldiers, helped Simon lift the cross and get it on his shoulders. There's no real conflict between the two accounts. Clearly Simon lifted the cross. He just didn't lift it alone.

We too are called to take up a cross. Some think of a cross as whatever hardship or difficulty life brings them. It may be a physical illness, financial want, or an agonizing accident. It may be racial prejudice, gender inequality, or social bias. Whatever it is, they are to bear it with dignity and courage.

Truly taking up our cross means dying to everything else. Simon had to put down what was in his hands, give up his destination, surrender his time, and spend his strength to carry that cross. There was no way for him to carry the cross and hang on to anything else. The same is true for us. We cannot embrace the cross while we grasp at other priorities, desires, and dreams. Many have tried. None have succeeded.

An engaged life isn't theoretical. It isn't hope or aspiration alone. It cannot be known without stepping into that life. No matter how risky it seems or how tentative our first steps, we cannot know life to the fullest without acting on that call.

Stage 5: New Priorities

Those who take up the cross can't go on living the same way or striving for the same goals. The expectations of our families, cultures, times, and our own desires are the well-worn path most follow. Following the cross means setting different goals and letting go of the lives we thought and dreamed about. Time and energy are the finite currency of life. When spent they are gone forever. In the end we run out of both.

To carry his cross means investing our lives in his cause, not ours; in his kingdom, not ours; and for his glory, not ours. We die to self long before we die. No one can carry our cross for us. It's ours and ours alone. But others help us lift the burden and sustain us along the way.

To live the life of a devoted follower of Christ doesn't mean giving up everything. It means being willing to give up anything that keeps us from knowing and following Christ with all we are.

Stage 6: Follow

Simon carried the cross behind Jesus. He followed. Perhaps Simon had been in Jerusalem many times or perhaps this was his first trip. In either case, it's not likely he had climbed the rocky path to Golgotha before. It was an awful place. The dead rotted on their crosses. When their decaying bodies fell to the ground, their bones were gnawed on and scattered by feral dogs and other animals. What was left was unceremoniously gathered up and thrown into the city garbage dump. All Simon could do was follow an unfamiliar path to an unknown destination and face an unknown destiny.

Simon didn't need to know the way or what would happen when he got there. All he had to do was focus on the man in front of him and go where he led. The rest would take care of itself. The Christian life is a lot like that. Those who follow Christ often don't know how, where, or what, but we always know who. We must focus on the one leading us. He knows the way. We do not know what will happen when we get there. He knows and has made sure that we will survive and thrive. Trust is our greatest need. That we can trust him is the greatest truth.

The trek up Golgotha was long and difficult. There was no joy or satisfaction in lugging another man's cross to his execution. Simon didn't want to be part of that travesty. Long before they reached Golgotha, Simon was tired, thirsty, and hurting. He wanted nothing more than to put the cross down, turn around, and go back into Jerusalem.

Those who take up Christ's cross can find themselves in similar straits. The burden is heavy and the road is long. Sometimes they experience disappointment, persecution, opposition, or sacrifice with little or no apparent reward. At some point they may want to drop the burden, turn around, and head back to the comfort and ease of life without the cross.

What keeps them on that road, what keeps them following Jesus in spite of every obstacle? It's not an easy question but some things seem clear.

We are convinced that God's word is truth. This world, for all its shining allure, is an illusion. The life God promises at the end of our burden-laden journey is ultimate truth.

A love for God drives us on. It springs from the rich soil of his love, grace, and forgiveness. Given what he did for us, there is no burden too heavy or journey too long and difficult.

A love for people compels us. We do not live selfish, self-focused lives. Others link arms with us and together we limp toward the higher calling of Jesus Christ.

We know what's at stake if we fail. Our lives and eternity are at risk. Failure emits deadly ripples that poison the lives of those we love and those we never know.

We draw on the power and presence of God's comforting Spirit. He sustains and strengthens us through the difficulties.

Journey's End

The Bible never mentions Simon again. We don't know how long he stayed at Golgotha or what he did after that awful morning. The only tantalizing tidbit of the future is Mark's reference to Simon's sons, Rufus and Alexander, who were obviously known to the church (Mark 15:21). We don't know if the believers named Rufus (Romans 16:13) and Alexander (Acts 19:33) were Simon's boys. If they were, we identify another feature of an engaged life: the man's influence on others and the future.

Simon was a bystander, a mere spectator who moved from the nameless, faceless crowd and became an active participant in the greatest story ever told.

Our circumstances aren't the same but our opportunity is. The irresistible and unstoppable truth of the crucified and resurrected Savior of humankind moves relentlessly through the world. Most are mere bystanders. It doesn't have to be that way. All we need to do is step into his story. When we do we find our story.

Easter reminds us that God refuses to be a bystander in human history and ignore human suffering and needs. We rejected him and rebelled. We bring suffering to each other, destruction to his creation, and misery to our own lives. But his love compelled him to step into human history, to become one of us and rescue us from ourselves. God is not silent, passive, or distant. God reaches down to comfort us and help us carry our burdens. He is not a bystander but a friend who welcomes all who come. Easter shines a bright light on that stunning truth.

St. Max, 2011

April 17—Palm Sunday
April 22—Good Friday
April 24—Easter Sunday

S ean invited me to Palm Sunday Mass at the Federal Correctional Institution and I went. He said the bishop was going to preach and I'd like it. He did. I did.

When I walked into the large room in the education wing that doubled as a chapel for the Protestants, Jews, Catholics, Muslims, and the host of other prison religions I noticed a large gold-on-red movable banner reading *"Welcome to St. Max"* in ornate script. I knew Catholics often named churches for a saint, but I had never heard of a Saint Max.

After the Mass, the inmates milled around the chapel until they could go back to their units. Several, including Sean, thanked me for being there.

"Thanks for coming, Doc. It means a lot," Sean said.

"You're welcome. I enjoyed it. Hey, who's St. Max? I've never heard of him."

"Really? I thought everybody knew about St. Max, patron Saint of Prisoners. He was murdered in Auschwitz. It's quite a story. He was a real Christian!"

The guards "called the move," which meant the inmates had ten minutes to move around the prison grounds.

"Sorry Doc, gotta get back to the unit. I don't want to get stuck here."

"No problem, Sean. See you Tuesday."

On the drive home, I turned Sean's words over and over in my mind. What kind of man drew such open admiration from a federal inmate doing a fifteen-year bit for armed robbery, attempted murder, and assault? I made up my mind to find out.

The Nazis arrested Father Maximilian Kolbe, a Polish priest, and sent him to Auschwitz for his stand against the invaders. On August 4, 1941, the camp's commandant chose ten prisoners to be starved to death as punishment for the presumed escape of another prisoner. One of the ten, Franciszek Gajowniczek, begged for his life for the sake of his wife and children. Kolbe stepped forward, offered to take his place, and joined those condemned to a slow, agonizing death. Kolbe prayed with and comforted the starving men and performed Last Rites when the time came. On August 14, Kolbe, the last of the ten, was executed by lethal injection. His body was unceremoniously cremated like those who went before him and the thousands who followed.

On Tuesday Sean came by my cramped office.

"Did you find out about St. Max?" he asked.

"Yes. It is an amazing story. He was a great man. But you called him a 'real Christian.' What did you mean?"

"Hundreds of men were willing to let other men starve to death. They just stood there, glad it wasn't them. But St. Max did something about it. Most people are more interested in themselves than anybody else. I was. It's why all of us are locked up in here."

I've thought often of my encounter with St. Max. A real Christian couldn't be a passive bystander watching a suffering and dying world. A real Christian is compelled to act in ways that honor Christ and serve others. Too many split theological hairs while the world around them goes to hell. Surely our Lord's command to "go into all the world" doesn't mean to go home, have Sunday dinner, watch the baseball game, and decry the sorry state of the planet. Surely it doesn't mean watching the parade of suffering from a safe distance. Surely Jesus meant for his followers to step into life, willingly sacrifice, and make a difference in the world.

Perhaps there is no such thing as an *innocent* bystander.

Chapter 8

The Death of Dreams

Pascha

7th Sunday in Lent—Easter

Introit

Confitemini Domino quoniam bonus quoniam in saeculum misericordia eius.
His steadfast love endures forever.

Psalm 118:1

Oh, give thanks to the Lord, for He is good! For His mercy endures forever.
Let Israel now say, "His mercy endures forever."
. . . The voice of rejoicing and salvation
Is in the tents of the righteous;
Psalm 118:1-2 (KJV)

There is no saint without a past, no sinner without a future.
—St. Augustine

His Little Girl

T he news spread like wildfire through the village. The miracle-working Rabbi from Nazareth was in Dalmuthea. It wasn't very far from their sleepy little fishing village—not far at all. Just next door, in fact.

The man made up his mind. He'd take his daughter to the Rabbi.

Years before, she had been wandering on the shore of the Sea of Galilee. She was just a child, abandoned, abused, and alone. The man and his wife had taken her in and raised her as their own. When she became a young woman the strange and frightening behavior began. So did their greatest agony. Their little girl was insane or demon-possessed or both.

But surrounding the Rabbi were stories about the blind seeing, the deaf hearing, and people freed from demons. What could it hurt? The father was desperate enough to try anything.

The next morning they walked together along the road that hugged the shore toward Dalmuthea. He looked across the mirror-flat surface of the lake and thought of that long-ago day when she came into their lives. It had been hard—especially these last few years. But he wouldn't have done anything differently. She was his daughter and he loved her.

"Where are we going, Father?" she asked.

"Dalmuthea."

"Why?"

"There is a man there I want you to meet," he replied.

"Are you arranging my marriage?" she asked with a hint of excitement in her voice.

"No, sweetheart—nothing like that."

"Then why?" Her disappointment was hard to miss.

"You'll see when we get there."

She knew not to press him for an answer he wasn't ready to give.

When they reached Dalmuthea the streets were full of excited people. They followed the crowd to the village square. A group of religious men—Pharisees, he thought—surrounded another man. Their voices were tense and harsh as they badgered him with questions and demanded answers.

He caught only part of the exchange but the Pharisees wanted the Rabbi to show them a sign from heaven—to prove he was the Messiah.

He heard part of the Rabbi's answer:

"An evil and unfaithful generation searches for a sign. But it won't receive any sign except Jonah's sign." (Matthew 16:4a)

The Rabbi turned and walked away, leaving his chattering adversaries speechless.

It was he, the Rabbi from Nazareth. The man hurried his daughter along. His heart was pounding. They joined the small group of other followers and walked with them until they were well outside the village. Without warning the Rabbi stopped, turned, and looked directly at the fisherman's daughter with a gaze so intense the old fisherman could only look away.

The Rabbi stepped through the small crowd toward them. With every step the Rabbi took the fisherman's girl grew more agitated. She tried to pull away but the fisherman held on. The girl cursed him—dug her fingernails into his flesh. She ranted and raved in a voice that was hers and not hers at the same time. She twisted and writhed, screamed and sobbed. It was all the fisherman could do to hang on to her. He never knew she was so strong.

"What do you want?" the Rabbi asked.

"Please teacher, my daughter. . . ."

What happened next was a blur.

"Come out!" The Rabbi's voice was calm, commanding, and compassionate. He gently touched the girl's shoulder. Her body stiffened. Her back arched. She threw her head back. She opened her mouth as if to scream and then suddenly she was limp and motionless at his feet.

Two of the Rabbi's followers helped the fisherman carry his little girl to a shady spot under some nearby trees. They said they were brothers named Peter and Andrew and had been fishermen just like him. The Rabbi sat near her and his followers stood in a tight circle around them.

"Will she be all right?" Her father was worried.

"She'll be fine," said the Rabbi.

"What was wrong with her?"

"Demons . . . seven demons."

The young woman stirred. She sat up and stretched as if waking from a long and restful sleep. Her eyes were clear and danced with a sparkle her father had never seen before. She smiled and stood.

"Thank you, Rabbi."

The Rabbi just smiled.

"They're gone, aren't they?" she asked.

"Yes, they're gone—all of them."

"They won't come back?"

"No. Not if you don't let them," the Rabbi answered.

"Father," she said, turning to him, "I want to go with him."

Of all the things her father thought would happen, of all the things he hoped and feared would happen—this had never crossed his mind.

One of his disciples gestured to a woman standing just outside the circle of his disciples. The woman said, "My name is Susanna—that's Joanna. She's married to Cuza, Herod's manager. Jesus healed her son. Maybe you heard about that? That's Salome. Over there is Mary. Those two just behind her are her boys, James and John. We follow the Rabbi and help out any way we can."

She read the fear in his eyes. "Don't worry. We'll look after her."

"What is your name, dear?" Susanna asked the young woman.

"Mary."

"Good! Another Mary! That makes three. Did you know his mother's name is Mary too?" she asked with a warm smile.

"And where are you from, Mary?" Joanna asked.

"Not far. We're from Magdala," she answered.

Mary Magdalene

Matthew 28:1-10; Mark 16:1-11; Luke 24:1-12; John 20:1-18

Mary Magdalene came a long way from the small, sleepy Galilean fishing village of Magdala and a life wracked by demonic possession. She followed her deliverer on the long dusty treks through the Judean hills and the shores of the Galilee. She served him and his disciples in every way she could all the way to Jerusalem, Golgotha, and the garden tomb.

Jesus gave her a reason to live and a future—a great hope and a dream. He was the Messiah. She thought she knew what that meant. In a matter of a few hours it was all gone.

What do we do when dreams die? What should we do next? Is there anything left to do? Some try to drown their grief in drugs, alcohol, sex, pleasure, or wealth. Some walk through life like hollow shells. Some kill themselves quickly. Others do it slowly, but in the end they get their death wish.

The Power of Dreams

Dreams are powerful. Pursuing a dream, a great goal, pulls us into a life of purpose and progress, one where we find sanity and stability. Because they dream, people raised in poverty or the chaos of substance abuse become great athletes, skilled scholars, or effective leaders. They find freedom from the lives they had by pursuing the lives of their dreams.

Dreamers Are Free

Some leave behind the limited and confining horizons of their hometowns, their ethnic heritages, or their financial circumstances. Dreamers move beyond the limits others accept as insurmountable and through barriers that seem impenetrable. They refuse their prescribed destinies. They let go of the expectations of others and no longer hear the voices telling them what and who they should be; they follow the call of their dreams. Captured by the one, they are freed from the others.

Dreamers Grow

The road to our dreams is a journey of growth and discovery. We learn vital lessons about our world and what it means to live the kind of life we treasure. We discover what we never expected to find in ourselves. The richest and most vital lessons surprise us.

We experience what can never be experienced without chasing a dream even when it seems we are tilting at windmills. We come to places and are challenged to do things we would never encounter otherwise. Our dreams enrich life in untold ways and become part of the tapestry of who we were and what we become.

Dreamers Learn

Fellow dreamers bring inestimable value to our lives. We meet teachers who guide our steps, those who support our dreams and those who don't understand but encourage us anyway. They become a permanent part of our story, whether they live only in our memories or share our daily lives. They make the trip worthwhile and add value to our lives in deep and profound ways.

Dreamers Give

Dreamers are a gift to those around them. Their efforts, even when they fail, add value to the lives and work of others. It's rarely the contribution they want to make, but that doesn't mean it isn't valuable or worthwhile. They make dreaming possible for those touched by their lives and inspired by their dreams.

Dreamers Lose

We lose the false and impossible hopes that keep us from our dreams. We lose the myopic perspective on life that keeps us from seeing things as they can be rather than as they are. We lose fear of failure, the laziness of hopelessness, and self-serving, self-deceiving excuses. We cannot fulfill our dreams or complete the transformation into the people we long to be without these and other losses.

No great dream can be pursued and achieved without the:

- courage to take on challenges and face risks.
- determination to give great and sustained effort despite disappointments.
- humility to admit wrong and to change course.
- faith to reach for a dream and believe it can be achieved.

It's hard to measure the changes in Mary's life. But it's impossible to imagine that living through such momentous events would not change her.

Transformed by Our Dreams

Dreamers like Mary experience at least three kinds of changes.

1. Our Self-Perception

Mary encountered Jesus and it changed how she saw herself. Before she was a demon-possessed girl from a small village; after she was a valued disciple contributing to Jesus's life and ministry. Before she was hopeless and helpless; after she was filled with great expectations for her life and future. Before she had nothing to live for and little reason to dream; after she became an integral part of the greatest moment in history.

Dreamers see themselves in new and unimagined ways. A different person looks back from the mirror. Sometimes the change makes people better. Sometimes it doesn't. Sometimes the bitterness and pain of failure poisons the soul and transforms the gentle optimist into a pathetic pessimist. That we are changed isn't up for debate. How we change is up to us.

2. What We Can Do

We may be surprised at what we are willing to do to see our dreams come true. Sometimes we act in ways that are noble, courageous, and incredibly admirable. Other times we betray what is best in us, sacrificing character and pride to the strong tides of desire. That self-knowledge, both the dimensions of the good and evil in us, is a hard-won prize that shapes our future.

3. The World Around Us

Dreamers know the world is full of promise, possibilities, and magic. The world is a wondrous place where anything can happen. But for disappointed dreamers the world is a dark and foreboding place with destruction and danger lurking around every corner. Some pass through their dark night of despair blind to the light of hope and promise. Some walk that path and exult in the bright light of new life and possibilities and step out of the shadow's pain.

Mary's journey from Galilean demoniac to despair at Golgotha mirrors the arc many lives follow. She began at a place she wanted to leave behind—a place of torment. In a bright and shining moment she discovered a new life and a very different reality. It was a joy-filled and wondrous path she expected to follow the rest of her life. It didn't happen.

Dreamers face and overcome obstacles that block their way to the lives they seek. They believed the dream would be the story of the rest of their lives. They wanted it that way. Then the dream died. The question isn't whether or not dreams die. They do. It isn't whether or not dreaming is a foolish waste of time. It isn't. Nor is it a question of whether or not we should pursue our dreams. Dream-chasing is in our nature. We can't help it.

The question is, what do we do when our dreams die?

The Death of Dreams

Mary walked the path of all who face the death of dreams. She models a healthy way to move past the death to build a future and dream again.

Accept the New Reality

Mary was present the day screaming throngs of people laid palm fronds and their coats on the road as Christ rode into Jerusalem on a colt. The shouts of "Hosanna" echoed through every street and alleyway as Christ made his way to the temple (John 12:12-19). It was an exhilarating moment and the pinnacle experience of her time with Christ. He entered Jerusalem like his ancestor David and made it clear that he was indeed the long-awaited Messiah who would rid their land of the hated Romans and establish his just and glorious kingdom.

Well, that's what his followers thought.

Their dream was about to come true!

It didn't.

Nothing in the accounts of the Last Supper or Christ's arrest in Gethsemane indicates that Mary or the other women were present for those events. We have no idea when or how Mary heard of his arrest.

Wherever they were, whatever they thought, saw, or heard, it was a terrifying time. All their hopes and dreams slipped away in that one dark night as the Romans, Herod, and their own religious leaders conspired to kill the Son of God. In the morning the Romans began the long gruesome parade to Golgotha. Mary Magdalene, Mary (Christ's mother), and the other women wept and begged for his life. The streets were choked with angry, bloodthirsty men and women insulting Jesus and screaming for his crucifixion. Each step brought them closer to an unimaginable agony. Mary of Magdala watched Jesus—and her dreams—die in the most excruciating and humiliating way possible (Luke 23:27) and saw him buried (Mark 15:40-41).

She had to accept a new reality. Her life would not be what she had hoped.

Let Unworthy Dreams Go

Mary accepted the fact that the dream she dreamed, the future she longed for, died on the cross. The women followed the burial party to the grave so they could come back after the Sabbath. During the next days, Mary and the women did what grieving people have always done. They gathered what they needed to care for his body and honor the dead.

The death of a dream brings the same intense grief as the death of one dearly loved. First we deny the truth of our loss. We struggle to let go of the dreams that have guided and energized our lives even when we know the dream is dead. We are angry and bargain with the powers that be to resurrect our dreams. In the end we accept the fact that what we longed for will never happen.

All of life, every vista and aspect, was once filled by the dream. Our dreams painted the colors and hues of every day. When the dream dies, we are left with a blank canvas. So we hang on to what can never be. Life with a dead dream, we reason, is better than one with no dream at all—better than staring into the empty void of the future.

But the death of our dreams steals the energy needed to live the adventurous life of a dream-chaser. Surviving, not dreaming, takes center stage. We walk through our days with no higher purpose than our next breath, drained of the creativity, energy, and courage we need to pursue a new dream. But dreaming is in our nature. The trick is to know what dreams to hang on to and what dreams to let die. It's not easy.

We shouldn't let go because dreaming is hard. All great dreams are difficult.

We shouldn't let go because it hasn't been done before or some think it can't be done.

We shouldn't let go because our dream takes a long time, requires great sacrifice, stretches us to the very limits of our ability, or pushes us to the brink. Great dreams do all of that. They are the only dreams worth dreaming.

We shouldn't give up on the dreams God places in our hearts no matter how outlandish and seemingly impossible.

But there are dreams we should let go.

We should let go of dreams that drive us to destroy or damage others and ourselves.

We should let lesser dreams go in order to embrace higher and nobler ones.

No one should sacrifice family, spouse, or children to pursue wealth, power, fame, pleasure, or some other petty dream. It is irrational to trade real gold for fool's gold.

No dream that requires dishonesty or a breach of character is worth it.

No one should hang on to a dream when its time has passed. Unfulfilled dreams from one time of life should be given a decent burial.

No one should hang on to a dream that isn't worth what it costs.

No one should hang on to a fool's errand. We have all received great gifts. But we have not been given the same gifts or every gift. Dreaming of what we do not have the talent, ability, or opportunity to accomplish is a foolish waste. Better to dream of making the most of the gifts we have than to pursue what we don't have.

Honor and Grieve the Past

Mary honored the past as she came to terms with her loss. The death of one loved deeply and missed sorely is painful beyond measure. It must have been agonizing for Mary to go back to the garden tomb. Certainly it would have dredged up the raw emotions of Jesus's torture and death less than seventy-two hours before and forced her to relive the worst day of her life. Many could not—would not—make that trek. Only a few had the love, devotion, and courage to face that torture to give Christ their final gifts. None of Jesus's brothers or apostles was there.

It wasn't a long walk but it was an indescribably difficult journey. The women's trip to Christ's tomb was one of the greatest acts of love ever recorded. It framed their commitment to him. They had nothing to gain and everything to lose. Some dismiss their journey as a cultural obligation. Others lose sight of their actions in the blinding glare of Christ's resurrection. To some the story merely fills in some details of the first Easter. All these miss the wondrous love on display in the simple act of such great and pure devotion.

The women needed to go back to his tomb to let go and begin to heal. Hiding from our pain hangs our losses around our necks like that much-fabled albatross. The deep wounds in heart and soul cannot heal until we face them. A dangerous infection grows if we don't cleanse it by confronting the loss. The searing pain of staring the truth in the face pales in comparison to the chronic agony of failing to deal with it.

Mary and the other women went to the grave that morning with their final gift. Recognizing, revisiting, and reliving a failed dream is a painful but absolutely necessary step to laying claim to and being enriched by the experience. We can let go and move on, grateful for what we were given, and carry those gifts into a richer future. Whether we know it or not, whether we want to accept it or not, we need the gifts from the past for whatever comes next.

See the New Possibilities

Mary had a hard time with what she found at the tomb. Who wouldn't?

Mary faced the reality that the life she thought she would have had died along with Christ. What she didn't and couldn't see yet were the marvelous possibilities hidden in that tragedy.

The tomb was sealed and guarded by soldiers Mary hoped would help roll back the stone. The women planned to enter the tomb and attend to Jesus's body. Perhaps they needed to wash away the dirt that still clung to his skin, replace the shroud stained with his blood, add sweet-smelling spices to those Nicodemus brought, and rewrap the body. That's not what happened.

Instead of guards they met angels, one outside and one inside the tomb.

Instead of a tomb sealed shut, it was wide open.

Instead of his body, they found only the grave clothes.

Instead of going about their work, they stood dumbfounded at the entrance.

Instead of a chapter closing in their lives, a new and wonderful reality opened.

Christians celebrate this moment in art, music, and worship. The women didn't react that way at all. Their reaction was so typical, so ordinary it lends even greater credence to the story. There is no patina of religious legend here, just shocked, trembling, terrified women running as fast as they could out of a graveyard! It's exactly what we'd expect, a mixture of overwhelming fear and astonished joy.

Mary saw the open tomb and the grave clothes and spoke to an angel. She'd been told to deliver a very specific message, "Tell his disciples that he has risen from the dead" (Matthew 28:7). But when she found Peter and John she said, "They have taken the Lord out of the tomb, and we do not know where they have laid him" (John 20:2). No mention of the open tomb, the angel, or his empty grave clothes. Somewhere between the tomb and the disciples her logical, rational side took over. Who would believe the story she was supposed to tell? Maybe she wasn't sure she believed it. She told Peter only the absolutely indisputable facts: Jesus wasn't in the tomb and she didn't know where the body was. It was the truth, edited and repackaged for the real world.

Peter and John sprinted to the tomb, looked in, entered, and saw what Mary saw (without the angels) and then left. They "did not understand the Scripture, that Jesus must rise from the dead" (John 20:9-10). They didn't get it any more than Mary and the women. It was too utterly fantastic.

All who stand at the tomb of a dead dream risk being so blinded by the old that they cannot see that something new and greater is breaking into their lives. They risk losing sight of what can be in the glare of what was. We too need to hear and heed the wisdom of the angel:

Don't be afraid. Fear both blinds and binds. Standing on the verge of something new and unknown can be frightening. The pain of the past and the desire to stay safe and avoid new risks are a powerful neap tide pushing us into the safe harbor of what was. We have good reason to be afraid. The path before us is not sure or safe and is shrouded in the mists of uncertainty.

Remember the dreams that brought you to this place. Mary and the women were at the tomb because they had pursued a dream, not because it hadn't gone as they hoped. The dream may have died but the need to dream, the hunger to fulfill a great and noble destiny, lived on in them and lives in us all. It can be damaged, suppressed, ignored, and neglected but not destroyed.

Look for what can be, not to what was. In that place of death there was new life. Again and again the new emerges from the crucible of loss and the chrysalis of desperation. Resurrection life, new dreams, and amazing possibilities were sprouting in the graveyard of dreams if they would see them. Chained to what was, we miss the moment and the seeds of new life and future.

Believe the evidence. The women witnessed clear and indisputable evidence of the resurrection and a new reality that day, but they didn't believe or understand. So the angel took the extraordinary step of pointing out what was obvious: the tomb was empty and the risen Christ had left the grave clothes behind. With all of that evidence they still struggled to comprehend. Many won't see the crystal clear evidence that new life, new dreams, and new hopes are waiting to be grasped, embraced, and enjoyed. In the death of a dream are the seeds of a new and greater dream, if we will have it.

Trust a greater truth. The angel said, "See, I have told you" (Matthew 28:7 ESV). What we're seeing feels odd and out of place. For Mary, the evidence should have been enough. But it wasn't. It is far too easy to rationalize and ignore what we see. We are far too dependent on what others think and far too insecure to trust our own feelings.

We are likely to ignore new possibilities in life and listen to the voices of others who dismiss our dreams as utterly fantastic. Are we wrong to doubt ourselves and listen to wise and caring people? Of course not! Sometimes what we need most is reality therapy! Pointing out the hard truth is a great service and an act of great courage and love.

But there is another voice, the voice of the one who sent the angels to the tomb. When we dream his dreams, listen to his voice, and join his mission, all things really are possible. There are no hopes or aspirations that come from God that cannot come true. God was at work that day and is at work every day. We live with the joyous guarantee that he brings to pass the good things he began in us and in our world.

God does not sync his clock with ours or run the world on our schedule. God's word assures and his character ensures that when we live his dreams for our lives they come true. He doesn't promise we'll live to see them. But that doesn't mean the dreams weren't true or not worth living. It means the opposite. It is the only truly worthwhile way to live *precisely because* those dreams are unbounded by our own limitations.

Discovering a New Dream

Mary followed the disciples and remained outside the garden tomb after Peter and John went home. The honor of being the first person to see the resurrected Christ belonged to a former demoniac named Mary Magdalene. Peter and John would have to wait. So would his mother, his brothers, the disciples, and all the others.

She took a second look into the tomb and saw the angels. One angel asked, "Woman, why are you crying?" (John 20:13)

There was a time for weeping. When Jesus was suffering and dying and hung limp and dead, waiting for a quick burial, they were right to weep. Sitting outside the tomb while Nicodemus and Joseph of Arimathea laid him to rest, they were right to weep. Mary wept because she believed his body had been stolen and hidden. She could not give him her final gift and would not have a place to mourn his death.

Then Mary saw a gardener. It was the only thing that made sense. She was still negotiating and desperately clinging to what she thought was the truth. But it was past time to stop focusing on the dead. It was time to celebrate and rejoice! There was no reason to weep!

In an instant and with a single word Mary discovered how to begin again.

Dream Forward

Mary encountered the future. The risen Christ opened the door to new and thrilling possibilities. There is no greater truth: life brings amazing opportunities without notice and without our permission, if we see them. Mary's old dream and its death no longer limited her future. The new reality was immense beyond imagination.

Find the Future

At his crucifixion Mary faced a future she never imagined. At the open tomb Mary confronted possibilities she did not understand.

But when Mary met the resurrected Christ, a new hope and future took shape.

All too many stop before they reach the end of this path. They can't see beyond their loss to new possibilities. Fear of pain and disappointment keep them from dreaming again even if they see new possibilities.

Up to that moment nothing convinced Mary that Jesus was truly alive. When he called her name something resonated deep in her soul. Mary began to experience the joy of her new life when she realized the gardener wasn't a gardener. Mary was awakened by his call. We too are called into new and marvelous lives if we will hear and answer. Vast and marvelous, the new realities are ours if we see them, if we waken to them.

Embrace the Future

Mary embraced the future. Crucified men don't come back from the dead. It cannot be true. But it was. Finding a new life and a new dream feels like that. What we never imagined, what we believed could not happen, happens. The opportunity is there. The door is unlocked and ajar. Some stand outside, peek through the crack, and long for what's inside but never cross the threshold. Others, like Mary, burst through and embrace what they find.

Mary threw herself into that moment with all the energy and excitement she could muster and embraced the miracle. She was neither timid nor reserved, and she did not hold back. She embraced the resurrected Christ and all his presence meant with every fiber of her heart, mind, and soul.

Mary could not have known all the future held. Persecution, suffering, and great challenges lay ahead. It wouldn't have mattered if she did. She found joy and freedom in that reckless abandon the careful and timid never experience. Little in life is more thrilling or fulfilling than to be overwhelmed with a great dream and swept along by its power and grandeur.

Act on the New Reality

Mary acted. Jesus wanted Mary to engage in the compelling mission of a new reality and sent her to his disciples to tell them what she had seen, heard, and experienced. Mary let go of the moment of elation and took up a life of mission. Moving past the romance of the dream and into the reality of making that dream come true is especially fulfilling.

What happened next is beautiful for its simplicity. The Bible says, "Mary Magdalene went and announced to the disciples, 'I have seen the Lord'—and that he had said these things to her" (John 20:19). That's all. It is the last time Mary Magdalene is mentioned and the last words we hear her speak in the Gospels. She expressed the most significant and deepest truth of her life in those five simple words: "I have seen the Lord."

Mary crossed the threshold from old to new, from death to life, and from past to future. She had seen the risen Lord and would never, ever be the same. Dreamers of great dreams never are.

The Same Lord, the Same Love

There is stunning continuity between the dream that died and the dream Mary discovered. Christ was still her Lord and love. Mary could not know the wonder of the resurrection and the extraordinary future that awaited her until her old way of seeing Jesus died. It was far too small to see the true dimensions of his life and work.

Our dreams are still our dreams. The dimensions change, are reshaped, and take on a new form. The passions that fueled the one fuel the other. The call of the old dream echoes in the new. The hard lessons of the first inform and shape the next.

Mary spent the rest of her life giving shape to the hopes, dreams, and aspirations of her resurrected and living Messiah. One has to wonder if she looked back at their hopes before Golgotha, amazed at how little she understood and the paltry and unworthy nature of those dreams. Did she come to the conclusion that the best thing that ever happened to her happened on the worst day of her life?

All who experience the death of a dream and discover a new and vibrant life end up glad the old dream died. The dream they live now is so much better. Others spend entire lifetimes wandering in the wastelands of dead dreams, mourning their losses. What's the secret? What makes the difference?

The Bible is full of stories of people whose dreams died but who still went on to live extraordinary and magnificent lives. Their dreams and circumstances were vastly different but a single thread runs through their stories: they let go of their dreams and lived in God's dreams for them.

Our best dreams are pale shadows of the great things God wants for us. That shouldn't surprise us. He created us. Our dreams reflect the passions and personalities he gave us. But dreams that are paltry and unworthy of his image must die if we are to encounter the wonders of his great dreams.

Mary Magdalene disappears from scripture after she carried the good news of Christ's resurrection to his doubting, frightened, and desperate disciples. We don't know what happened to her. There are legends, speculations, and stories but no true history. But we can be sure Mary fully engaged the great mission of the Lord she loved and served. Mary lived her greatest dreams until the day she died.

Will we? It's up to us.

Easter means we can dream again. The doubting, discouraged, and despairing find new hope in the one who conquered death to bring everlasting life. Easter means we can dream of what can be and be freed from what was. Easter means we can dream of knowing a life that is full and rich and meaningful. Easter means we can find purpose for our lives and joy in living. We know that when we discover and embrace God's dreams for our lives, they will come true. Dreamers are welcome on the road to the cross.

Their Little Girl, 2003

April 13—Palm Sunday
April 17—Good Friday
April 20—Easter Sunday

Easter came late that year and Alaina was three months into a picture-perfect pregnancy. Everything was going just right and she and her husband, Kelly, couldn't have been happier. One afternoon, following a routine ultrasound, the phone rang. It was their obstetrician asking them to come in for some tests. The doctor didn't like what she'd seen on the ultrasound and wanted to make sure everything was all right.

They had the tests, another ultrasound, and waited. On June 18 they sat in the doctor's office and heard the worst news of their lives. Their baby had a genetic abnormality called Trisomy 18, or Edwards Syndrome. The doctor explained that the syndrome was very rare and afflicted mostly little girls. Their baby would be born horribly deformed and die before or shortly after birth.

"We recommend you terminate the pregnancy," her doctor said. "I'll have the nurse set up the procedure as soon as possible."

"Terminate? You mean have an abortion?" Alaina asked.

"Yes. But don't worry. The procedure is safe. You're young and strong. There is nothing wrong with either of you and there is no reason you can't have other healthy children."

Kelly asked the doctor to excuse them so they could talk. She left the room. The young couple cried and prayed and talked and came to a decision.

When the doctor came back she handed Alaina the paperwork needed to terminate the pregnancy. "It's set up. All we need is your signature," she said.

"No. We're not having an abortion," Kelly said. "Yes. We believe God can heal our little girl. We're going to give God a chance to do a miracle. If he doesn't, she's still our little girl and we'll love her for as long as we have her."

That was the end of it.

On July 14, 2003, Hope Elizabeth was stillborn. She came into this world with all the cruel abnormalities the doctor predicted. Her mother and father and grandparents dearly loved and grieved her. They held her, talked to her, sang to her, prayed with her, and told her how much she was loved. She passed into the loving arms of Jesus and never knew fear, sickness, or pain.

They had hoped and prayed but there was no miracle. They were not spared the agony of her tragic death and their loss. But Alaina and Kelly never regretted their decision.

A year after Hope's death Alaina and two other women who had lost children started Tiny Purpose, a ministry to families who have lost infants. It wasn't the miracle they hoped and prayed for, but it was a miracle. Through a growing network she and other women reach out to love and comfort others in their time of suffering. Tiny Purpose is a fitting legacy for one little girl who was deeply loved, too soon gone, and sorely missed. It was the least they could do for her. After all, she was their little girl.

Alaina's mother and father created a ministry that bears Hope's initials, HEH, which stands for Hope and Encouragement for Humanity. The organization focuses on hunger and disaster relief. Since Hope's death, HEH has distributed hundreds of tons of food and relief supplies to some of the world's most hurting people. It's part of the legacy of one little girl who continues to touch and comfort those experiencing great need and suffering. It seemed like the least they could do.

After all, she was their little girl too.

Tiny Purpose

357 Sherman St.

Blissfield, MI 49228 (517) 486-2140

www.tinypurpose.com

Hope and Encouragement for Humanity
631 Depot St.
Blissfield, MI 49228
(517) 486-3285
www.h-e-h.org

Epilogue

Bit Players

Remember: there are no small parts, only small actors.
—Constantine Stanislavski

Other minor characters appear in the Easter story, others were on the road to the cross: the servant girls who challenged Peter, Pilate's wife, the man who loaned Jesus the donkey on Palm Sunday, and the owner of the Upper Room. Hundreds who were in Jerusalem for that Passover went home with their own accounts of Christ's death and the events that followed. For many, it had little or no impact on their lives.

Named and unnamed men and women are included in the Gospel narratives for a reason. Each of them has a unique place and each sheds light on an aspect of the Gospel story.

Simon the Leper and the sinful woman in Capernaum teach us that no one is beyond the love and acceptance of God's great love. He is and always has been the God of the outcasts.

Malchus teaches us that Christ has no enemies except those who will not be his friend.

The centurion reminds us that we are at war with our world and our will. We find true peace only in surrender to the God who created us.

Cleopas reminds us that we are all on a road to somewhere or to nowhere. Only an encounter with God can show us the way home.

Nicodemus and Joseph of Arimathea challenge all who pretend to be what they are not to rather live with authenticity and integrity.

Pilate shows us how we make our own prisons. Barabbas reminds us that no matter how thick our chains or deep our dungeon, Jesus can and will set us free, if we let him.

Simon the Cyrene teaches us that in the cause of Christ there is no such thing as an innocent bystander. If we are bystanders we are not innocent.

Mary Magdalene reminds us that there is no place so dark that the light of Christ's love cannot penetrate, nor past so horrible that a bright future is not possible.

Their stories remind us that we are like them.

All too often we think we have nothing significant to contribute to the world. But we too have stories to tell. Like these men and women, we are here for a purpose. It may not seem like much in the great sweep of history, but it matters. Our influence, our love, and our gifts matter to others and to the future.

Whether we know it or not, we see it or not, others see Easter through our eyes. We can help set captives free, heal the wounded, and welcome the outcast. We can help people find peace, live with integrity, and fulfill their dreams. We can walk with those who are lost and help them find their way home.

We may feel we've been asked to play a small part in the great drama of God's work in the world. But we should give an Oscar-worthy performance with all the joy and enthusiasm it demands. We have been given the key that unlocks a happy ending for those we love, those we influence, and ourselves: new life in Christ.